Women in the Wilderness

Augustin Roussin

M'à feict dans la uille de marseille

WOMEN IN THE WILDERNESS

China Galland

HARPER COLOPHON BOOKS

HARPER & ROW, PUBLISHERS

NEW YORK, CAMBRIDGE, HAGERSTOWN, PHILADELPHIA, SAN FRANCISCO

LONDON, MEXICO CITY, SÃO PAULO, SYDNEY

Grateful acknowledgment is made for permission to reprint:

Excerpt from *The Dream of a Common Language, Poems 1974–1977*, by Adrienne Rich. Copyright © 1978 by W. W. Norton & Company, Inc. Reprinted by permission of the publisher and author.

Excerpts from "Little Gidding" in *Four Quartets* by T. S. Eliot. Copyright 1943 by T. S. Eliot; copyright 1971 by Esme Valerie Eliot. Reprinted by permission of Harcourt Brace Jovanovich, Inc.

"Climbing Aconcagua" by Frances Mayes in *After Such Pleasures* (New York: Seven Woods Press, 1979). Reprinted by permission of the author.

Picture credits appear on page 162.

WOMEN IN THE WILDERNESS. Copyright © 1980 by China Galland. All rights reserved. Printed in the United States of America. No part of this book may be used or reproduced in any manner whatsoever without written permission except in the case of brief quotations embodied in critical articles and reviews. For information address Harper & Row, Publishers, Inc., 10 East 53rd Street, New York, N.Y. 10022. Published simultaneously in Canada by Fitzhenry & Whiteside Limited, Toronto.

FIRST EDITION

Designed by Bonnie Carpenter

Library of Congress Cataloging in Publication Data

Galland, China.
    Women in the wilderness.
    (Harper colophon books; CN 817)
    Bibliography: p.
    Includes index.
    1.   Outdoor recreation for women—Addresses,
essays, lectures.   I.   Title.
GV191.64.G34   613.6'9   80–7830
ISBN 0–06–090817–3 (pbk.)

80 81 82 83 84 10 9 8 7 6 5 4 3 2 1

To my children, Matthew, Madelon and Benjamin

Contents

Acknowledgments

I would like to express my special thanks for assistance in writing this book to Stephanie Mills, whose careful editing of the several drafts improved the book substantially. Her help and friendship were critical in writing this book. Karen Otsea came to me as a student intern and performed a variety of tasks far beyond the original research phase and was invaluable in her help and friendship. Susan Griffin greeted my ideas warmly and introduced me to Bonnie Carpenter, who then took my ideas for a "rutter" and transformed them into a workable book design. Stephanie, Karen, and Bonnie all maintained unfailing good humor and support at critical junctures in the project when I most needed their help. Martha Glessing and Monica Suder both contributed by helping me see ways to balance writing, working, and pulling together the book visually. Thanks also to Ann Roberts for her part in helping me to complete the book. Chikīdō Lew Richmond-sensai of the San Francisco Zen Center read the manuscript to see that my beginner's grasp of Buddhism fell within the scope of more formal teachings. Jean Caldwell typed drafts on her days off and encouraged me a great deal. Karen Allen, who typed the final manuscript, deserves thanks for her patience in deciphering my revisions. Jerry Bagger and Vince Genovese of Gamma Photo in San Francisco and Karen Spagenberg provided invaluable assistance in assembling and printing many of the photographs. AKA Fox of Albany's Carbon Alternatives provided important help at key moments. Janet Goldstein and Ruth Bornschlegel of Harper & Row are to be thanked for seeing the book through its final stages. Particular appreciation goes to Hugh Van Dusen, my editor at Harper & Row, who believed in the project in the first place.

Some of the items for which I give thanks were simply small deeds in the long, drawn-out process of producing a book. But the timing and the care with which they were executed, the good humor when my own was sorely tried, the enthusiasm, and the criticism were all part of writing this book; without everyone's help it would not have come into being. In addition, other writers and women who inspired me, my colleagues, friends, and acquaintances in Women in the Wilderness are all a part of the context from which this book grew, and can never adequately be thanked. Rosalie Moore, Barbara Hazilla, Sandy Walter, Mia Monroe, Judy Irving, and the other members of the board of directors I appreciate for sharing a vision of what Women in the Wilderness is now and might become.

My brother, Chris Walters, my children, Matt, Madelon, and Ben, to whom I've dedicated this book, my families both immediate and former, have all been supportive in innumerable ways. Finally, I owe a great deal of thanks to Tyrone Cashman, whose friendship and alliance continually helped me find a way to persevere and complete this work.

For if we think of this existence of the individual as a larger or smaller room, it appears evident that most people learn to know only a corner of their room, a place by the window, a strip of floor on which they walk up and down. Thus they have a certain security. And yet that dangerous insecurity is so much more human which drives the prisoners in Poe's stories to feel out the shapes of their horrible dungeons and not be strangers to the unspeakable terrors of their abode. We, however, are not prisoners.

—RAINER MARIA RILKE

Introduction

This book contains accounts of some of my own wilderness experiences as well as those of other women. At its best it reveals moments which have touched and shaped a life, the poetry of significant experience. It also serves as an informal history of an organization by the same name, Women in the Wilderness, which was begun in 1975 by a handful of women and myself.

This book is primarily about women you will not have heard of. Though there are a few women mentioned who are famous, most are not. There are many more who could have been included, but I write only of those with whom I have had personal contact or of historical figures whose stories have touched me for one reason or another. "Why this story, this woman?" one might ask. I am reminded of walking along a pebble-strewn beach in sandals and finding a small stone stuck in my shoe. There are thousands of pebbles that I've walked over, but the one that is stuck in my shoe compels me to stop, remove it, perhaps examine it for a moment, and then toss it away. These chapters reflect some of the pebbles that have made me stop for a moment along the way.

Eastern wisdom holds that the obstacle is the path. This telling transforms stone to story. Compiling these notes from my journey was my bending over, pulling out the stone, and holding it up to the light. Your reading is the toss back into the ocean, where it will quietly sink and settle among a thousand other stones.

This book is cast in the form of a rutter, a book kept by a ship's pilot for navigation in the days before there were reliable maps of the world in the thirteenth through the sixteenth centuries. Each chapter is titled as an entry in a rutter.

Rutters were comprehensive logs of routes, kept by the pilots of the experience of the journey. They included charts of the coast and drawings and renderings of harbor entrances, islands offshore, and rocks to beware of. Sometimes the actual charts were separate, though used

DIRECTIONS FOR SAILING
USED IN RUTTERS

North: "toward the dark"
South: "toward the light"
Northeast: "summer sunrise"
Northwest: "summer sunset"
Southeast: "winter sunrise"
Southwest: "winter sunset"

in conjunction with a narrative account of the route to be followed. They contained distances between safe harbors and, more important, the direction to sail, for without good direction, one never arrived at all. They might contain numerous notes in the margins, indicating the depth of the water, native plants to be found, weather encountered, phases of the moon, the variety of trees along the shore; describing local customs, neighbors, causes of political strife in the life alongshore, shifts in weather, storms encountered; speculating on the color of the seas; including names of cities and towns to be discovered along the route, the occasion of the voyage itself, and a welter of explanatory remarks. Notation probably was limited only by the pilot and his range of interest. Rutters were compiled during the period of great geographical discoveries, the thirteenth through the sixteenth centuries. Called *portolanos* by the Catalonians and Italians who initially developed them, they were known as *routiers* in French, *roteiros* in Portuguese, and *rutters* in English.

The sixteenth-century portolan chart at the front of this book gives you an idea of the accuracy with which the world had been charted by those who sailed it. Remember that it was drawn from first-hand observation only. The almost scientific accuracy of rutters is remarkable and made them highly prized. Many maps were drawn in the cloisters of the Middle Ages, but while notable for their aesthetic value, their inaccuracies are in marked contrast to the charts made by the navigators and chart makers who worked from the sea itself.

Though few original rutters remain from this period, I was able to find two of them and a portolan chart in various rare book departments, and I gleaned enough from the history of cartography to compile these characteristics. James Clavell's definition of a rutter in his novel *Shogun* is also useful here:

A rutter was a small book containing the detailed observation of a pilot who had been there before. It recorded magnetic compass courses between ports and capes, headlands and channels. It noted the sounding and depths and the color of the water and the nature of the seabed. It set down *how we got there and how we got back:* how many days on a special tack, the pattern of the wind, when it blew and from where, what currents to expect and from where; the time of the storms and the time of fair winds; where to careen the ship and where to water; where there were friends and where there were foes; shoals, reefs, tides, havens; at best, *everything* necessary for a safe voyage. . . .

But a rutter was only as good as the pilot who wrote it, the scribe who hand-copied it, the very rare printer who printed it, or the scholar who translated it. A rutter could therefore contain errors. Even deliberate ones. A pilot never knew for certain *until he had been there himself.* At least once.

A rutter might contain errors deliberately inserted as a device to prevent others from discovering a trade route, often to the East, in case a ship fell into another country's hands. Many ships were lost at sea because of inaccurate directions and the wrap of secretiveness which surrounded these books. They must have been intensely personal and idiosyncratic.

But in truth you can never be certain of the directions on a map or found in a rutter unless you have been there yourself, experience being the most, if not only, reliable guide. This rutter is based on my own experiences, some of which may be useful to you, some of which may not. It would be unwise to follow the same route, though in its description you may recognize a similar landscape, find a direction, or see a landmark on the coastline that helps you chart your own journey.

The way for us is not mapped. Each journey yields more clues. We are still in the days of exploring, observing the landscape and the shoreline, making notes, compiling rutters. Whether discovering a route or making a trail, it is essential to remember that the rutter that falls into your hands or the path you find marks another's way. It is not your own. To find your own path, you must enter the forest alone in the dark, set sail in the night.

There is ice plant along the shoreline, monterry cypress; anemones and mussells cover the rocks. We find wild mustard and anise. There are willows, sword ferns, accacia, and eucalyptus.

Being a woman has too often been defined as what is the opposite of man. Categories of masculine and feminine behavior inhibit us, women and men, one and all, and prevent us from identifying with one another as human beings, sharing the fate of existence. We imagine that we are separate, that each is the "other." In our delusion we turn on one another rather than within ourselves. The separation is illusory; we are different, but we are not other; we are alone, but not separate from the world of nature, from each other.

Most of what we have now is a record of the world as experienced and perceived by men. It is valid. Yet there is something missing: the world as perceived by women, out of our own experience rather than as defined in opposition to masculine experience. This rutter is a record of a length of coastline I have traveled as a woman.

Someday, as the cartographers did with rutters after hundreds of years, we can put our notes and charts together and find before us revealed whole continents and vast oceans. Then we will be able to see a variety of ways to navigate these seas, numerous directions to set off in; we will have maps. But, in order to use a map, you must already be able to locate yourself, know where you are. For us that will come later. We are still in the process of discovering routes, exploring who we are.

*The rules
break like a thermometer,
quicksilver spills across
the chartered systems,
we're out in a country that has no
language, no laws, we're chasing
the raven and the wren through
gorges unexplored since dawn.
Whatever we do together is pure
invention, the maps are out of
date by years . . .*
          —ADRIENNE RICH,
    "The Dream of a Common
              Language"

The journey we make, the route we seek, is toward wholeness, toward our humanity. But we can start only where we are, from inside our own skins, in our own backyards. Hence this book focuses on my experience as a woman. The differences between men and women are more epistemological than sexual. We *perceive* the world differently. Both modes of perception are valid, and truth, if it can be said to reside anywhere, exists in the interplay between the two, not in one or the other.

In growing up, I only made a partial identification with the world around me. I didn't know, or only heard of women who lived outside of the traditional model of female. The need to run wild, the sense of adventure and exploration, the excitement in discovering the world of nature around me were not acceptable in a grown woman. These I was supposed to leave behind. Madison Avenue, *Playboy* magazine and Wall Street had a different image in mind. Sexuality was distorted and wildness confined to the bedroom. I could not recognize or accept the image of woman depicted by our society. It was at odds with what I knew and yet a part of the culture that created the image. No one is innocent. So I struck out on my own.

But don't be fooled by the romance of faraway places that you'll find in this story. There have been many times when the going was rough and I was driven into the wilderness to make sense of a life that didn't fit.

Meeting Randi Dubois, Anne Styron, Erica Fielder, Sandi Mardigian, Tracy Gary, and Kat Kipping marked a turning point over the last few years, created an avenue, the organization of Women in the Wilderness. Here were other women who cared for the wilderness, spent time in it, needed to lead their own lives.

Initially meeting informally around a kitchen table to talk and plan outings, we quickly grew by word of mouth, began a newsletter, created a network.

We defined ourselves, became a nonprofit tax-exempt corporation designed to support women becoming leaders of their own lives as well as in society through experiences in the wilderness. Our sense of kinship with the environment grew. The idea was working for us, maybe it would for other women too. We've kept the organization open to men, have trips that are open to men from time to time, though leadership must always be by women. This is the one stipulation. When women become leaders in the wilderness, preconceptions and stereotypes fall by the wayside, for us all. Women are seen in leadership roles that demand competence, boldness, courage, a willingness to take risks, a sense of adventure. It's new for both women and men to rely on a woman in this capacity. We see ourselves as an inclusive rather than exclusive organization.

Over the last five years as a volunteer organization we have grown to a thousand members around the country. Our publication carries news of trips led by women, some open to women only, some to mixed groups. We run a jobs clearinghouse for women who want work involving the outdoors. We are developing an environmental forum to heighten members' awareness of our environment. We're still growing, changing, moving from being a volunteer group to the necessities of paid staff, developing a more solid program grounded in the realities of today's fragile world.

Going into the wilderness invokes the wildness within us all. This may be the deepest value of such an experience, the recognition of our kinship with the natural world. Paradoxically this is the most human aspect and the most difficult to describe. Here we move into a realm where language breaks apart like logs in a beaver dam hit by a swollen wall of mountain water in the spring. In this rutter you will find some notes transcribed from my journals and trip logs, records of a past. Yet as I write the present always intrudes, like another layer of color, darkening the first impression, obscuring a hillside there, changing a shape, until I no longer recognize the entry before me and I am in another country, exploring rivers of woods, oceans of forests, lost in the stream of the mind. Language cannot contain the movement of the spirit, but it affords us a tracing.

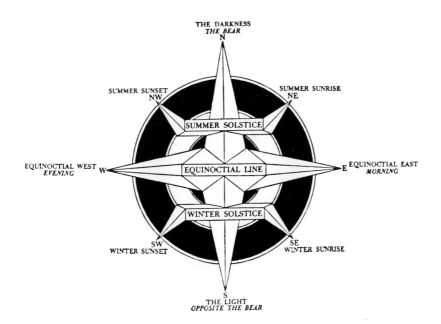

I   The Color of the Water

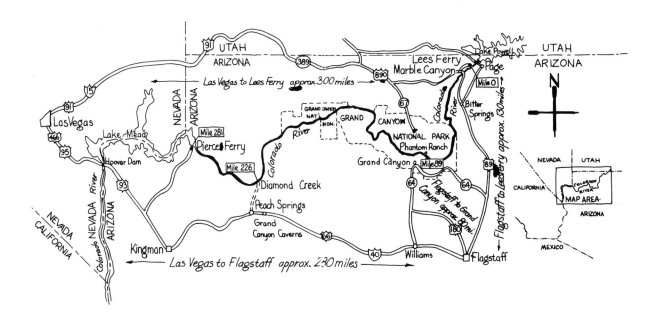

I

The Color of the Water
first all-women's Grand Canyon rafting trip

THE ABYSMAL (WATER)

Water sets the example for right conduct.
. . . It flows on and on, and merely fills
up the places through which it flows; it
does not shrink from any dangerous spot
nor from any plunge, and nothing can
make it lose its own essential nature.

—I CHING

ugust, 1978: Carol Schneier is rowing. It is hot, 115 degrees. She asks someone to throw a bucket of water on her. I lean over the side of the raft with a bailer and pull up a bucket of the Colorado, temperature 52 degrees, and throw it on her from across the boat, wetting down a few more women in the process. The cold water revives her for the afternoon rowing. I dip in for another bucketful and pour it over myself. The trip has begun; it's been a year in the planning and organizing. The first all-women's rafting trip down the Grand Canyon.

Many other women have run the Canyon, starting in 1928 when Bessie Hyde drowned on her honeymoon at Mile 232 on the Colorado. She was the first woman on record to attempt the journey. Five years later, Alzada Clover, a botanist, and her student, Lois Jotter, became the first women to successfully run the Canyon. They were passengers on a trip with John Neville, the first commercial river runner on the Colorado. Georgie White Clark swam the rapids of the Colorado in a life jacket in 1945, and then again in 1946. She and her companion, Harry Aleson, were the first to attempt this feat. More than thirty years later, Georgie still runs the river, the only woman outfitter in the Grand Canyon. She pioneered running the Colorado, developing the use of big stable pontoon boats that allow you to run the big rapids. Until 1955, only about five hundred people had run the Canyon. After the developments made by Georgie, river running became increasingly popular. And yet, despite Georgie's success, women river guides continue to be the exception rather than the rule. Many Canyon outfitters

Lee's Ferry/Mile 0

refused to hire women except as cooks until the early 1970s.

During the summer of 1977, I finally had a chance to run the Canyon. I went on twenty-four hours' notice. A cousin from back East called wanting to come visit. I said, "Fine. How would you like to trade a plane ticket for two weeks' care of my children?" She agreed. I told her to get on the plane that night; the next morning I left for Arizona. I was hellbent to run that river. I felt that I was going under in the aftermath of a divorce. Being civilized became an impossibility. The only fit place for me was the wilderness—the wilder, the better.

There are no ceremonies for our grief at the end of a relationship, no funeral to acknowledge the powerful emotions that arise. When a person dies it is acceptable to wear black, to be unpredictably emotional. People gather round, send notes of condolence and flowers. But, when we divorce, we mistakenly expect to carry on our regular life despite the inner death that is occurring.

While on that first trip I discovered that one of my fellow passengers had brought along a *Playboy* magazine, theoretically because of an article on the Grand Canyon. The "article" turned out to be a series of photographs of nude bunnies being rowed down the Canyon by a male crew. I began joking with a woman river guide about running an all-women's trip in response. Before the trip was over, it was no joke. By the time I returned to California, I had discovered that no group of women had ever run the Canyon. Commercial outfitters had not thought of the idea. My friend Rob Elliott, who had been among the first to hire women guides in the Canyon, encouraged me. His company, ARTA, Southwest (now Arizona Raft Tours), was the only one with enough qualified women guides to run a full commercial trip. Rob and his partner, Jessie Elliott, agreed to co-sponsor the trip with Women in the Wilderness. The following pages are my notes from that trip.

DAY 1

Our put-in at Lee's Ferry in Arizona takes place alongside several other trips that are departing this same morning. Buses arrive and unload passengers, who mill around while those of us on the crews of the various companies assemble the boats, gear, and food for the next two weeks' rafting. The bus with our passengers is late. The five women and myself as crew have been working hard since first light. We put the boats together, inflating the pontoons, bolting together the splash boards, and lashing the rigs together. Then we pack the food, gear, and clothing on the three unwieldy "snout rigs," our twenty-two-foot oar-powered pontoon boats. The twelve-foot Avon paddle boat will carry only people, no gear. When we finish loading the pontoon boats, known as snout rigs, they will weigh two thousand pounds each. I am apprehensive about these extra-heavy loads. The boats are unwieldy to begin with.

Finally the bus arrives and women begin streaming off into the midmorning heat, already well over one hundred degrees by ten in the morning. A woman reporter and a cameraman from *Newsweek* appear to film our loading and departure. One by one our passengers arrive. People are curious: an all-women's trip? Our group is extremely diverse and all typecasting is rapidly melting in the heat of our meeting and the Arizona sun. Still I know that there must be a common thread that has drawn us all together. I am surprised, pleased again to find reality so much larger and more imaginative than I will ever be. No one fits my preconceptions. There are twenty-one participants and six crew members, making a total of twenty-seven women.

We continue to load our gear onto the boats, have a safety talk, wave to the cameras, and put in on the Colorado River. Those of us on the smaller paddle boat, curious about each other, begin to talk about why we've come on this trip. Lauren Crux had been hospitalized long ago with suspected bone cancer and had almost lost a foot. In the process of telling us her story, she discovers that this trip is a celebration of her recovery.

We row and paddle deeper into the Canyon; stories unfold down through the afternoon.

DAY 3

At our campsite we find Indian ruins and granaries in the cliff sides. This is my first morning of pumping up the boats and latrine duty. We carry all human waste out with us. I am both an assistant for ARTA on the boat crew and the trip organizer for Women in the Wilderness. It makes for an awkward role. I'm accustomed to being the leader, but on this trip that position is filled by a woman much more competent than I would be. Our chief river guide, Louise Hoagland, has run the Canyon over thirty-five times; there is little for me to do in terms of my usual role in a group. I decide to do nothing about my discomfort at this except to notice the difficulty in letting someone else run the show. This is an opportunity to relinquish a part I am forever playing, to let go. I choose the awkwardness of having no clearly defined role. I write and observe more. The teachings of Zen Buddhism come to mind: There is no past, no future, there is only *this* moment. Inevitably, it is different from my plan.

For a while today I row Suzanne Jordan's boat, admiring her ability to let me make my own mistakes. With the extra weight, the boat is unwieldy, slow to respond to any of my movements at the oars. I learn to look farther and farther downstream, to read the water not only in front of me but at a distance, and continually to make adjustments as I row. With the weight of the boat and the speed of the current, maintaining momentum is requisite; a last-minute move can save us

Middle Nankoweap/Mile 52

What a lot of abrupt and flowing transitions a river day contains. The recent one is from river current and paddles and eddies seeming the constant way of life, to the sudden buzzing domesticity of camp appearing . . . neighborhoods being defined . . . tasks of the social order replacing the demands of the river. But there will be the moment we get back into the boats tomorrow. For me the day was a spiral of strange coherence.

—JOY HARDIN

from hitting a rock, entering a rapid sideways, or getting sucked into an eddy. Suzanne coaches me: "Face the danger, face your obstacle, that's where the current is. Stay as close to the obstacle as possible, that's where the current is the strongest. Use it." The river demonstrates an elementary lesson. The natural world contains them all. And, of all the forces of nature, water is my most important teacher.

Unkar/Mile 73

DAY 5

The morning sky is crusty with stars. One shoots across the heavens here at the Indian ruins of Unkar. I bow to spirits of the Anasazi people who lived here, asking their blessings. Today we face several big rapids, one right after another, including Crystal, which is nearly as difficult as Lava Falls, the fastest navigable rapids in the world. Today is the test. I know if we do well there is nothing to be afraid of.

We run the rapids: Hance, Sockdologer, Horn, Granite, Hermit, and Crystal, no mishaps, all well done. All rate seven to nine on a scale of difficulty that stops at ten. I am high with the excitement; my laughter returns. I can see clearly Louise's boat below the first one through, waiting for us as we make our run in the paddle boat through Crystal. Everyone below is standing up, clapping. We are all shouting as the last boat, a snout rig running close behind us, comes through safely, clearing the enormous hole on the left which would have flipped the entire rig, passengers and all.

When we make camp late that afternoon, Lauren, who was with me in the paddle-boat crew, comments:

This place is intense, powerful, holy, erotic, stark, and lush, and always grand. I feel all of that in me at times here. Erotic, intense, laidback, funky, flowing, churning, churning, gurgling, powerful, weak, afraid, fearless, and on and on, the river keeps on flowing.

—LAUREN CRUX

"Incredible things happened to me today. At the first rapid I was so scared that I was about to throw up. After we went through that one I got excited; I felt strong and agile. I knew that I wasn't going to fall out of that boat. I had a tremendous sense of power and rhythm. Barb was yelling, saying that we were doing it perfectly, and I had that real elation of all of us as women working together, and it was hard and dangerous and we were not afraid. I had the sense of catching the world.

"And then, just after we cleared Crystal, the biggest one, in the flat water, I felt like crying. The Canyon is magnificent and holy and the experience we had together was holy. I have already had what I wanted out of this trip—women doing something powerful together, trusting each other and succeeding."

Elves' Chasm/Mile 116

DAY 6

Lorna, the other assistant guide on this trip, is twenty, works only outdoors, and when she's not in the Canyon, she might be off picking apples or doing construction work. She is small and lovely; also lithe and strong. I follow Lorna's lead and make this hike up to Elves' Chasm barefoot. My feet are tougher than I imagined, the ground cooler, and the rocks easier to climb and scramble up in my bare feet.

I rediscover a sureness in my movement as I clamber up over boulders, up canyon walls, across rock ledges. I find toe holds, finger holds, hand holds that I don't even see as I move up a steep face. I give myself some elementary climbing instructions: "Breathe." "Trust your feet." "Use your hands only for balance." I have to laugh at how often I forget them in my everyday life. I move up a steep rock ledge and become anxious and then realize that I am holding my breath. As soon as I catch myself and take another breath, the fear subsides, the anxiety lessens. I move on to the ledge above me.

In the natural world stress is understandable and obvious, consequences clear. It is no surprise to feel some anxiety when climbing a rock face, unaided, fifty feet off the ground; a fall could break your neck. The cause of tightness in the pit of my stomach is apparent, the results of a fall simple, distinct, and painful.

At the end of the climb, the trail takes us into a high box canyon, where a hundred-foot-high, thin waterfall flows. I walk up to the slow seeping wall behind the fall and press my whole body against its mossy surface, feeling that I have returned to an old friend in whom I can confide.

Later, I find a good sitting rock, pull out my watercolors and begin to paint. The more I paint, the more clearly I see the welter of detail in the surrounding world. The natural world is a phenomenon always receding beyond my grasp. I narrow my focus. Self-taught, I do not make realistic drawings with three dimensions. The drawing takes on a life of its own when I am able to let the line of a rock run through me onto the page without thinking about it.

DAY 7

Sue Hirschfield, thirty-eight, is an assistant professor of earth sciences at California State University at Hayward. Dr. Sue we call her affectionately. I can't imagine this trip without her. The Grand Canyon is a geologist's dream and Sue makes no attempt to mask her excitement.

Oceans, rivers, currents, sands, and sediments formed the layers of rock that we look at now. Because of Sue's interpretation I can see whole forests, valleys, and warm seas in the rock in front of me. This canyon was once filled with blue waters, palm trees, and hibiscus. The appearance of metamorphic rock in the side canyon means that entire mountain ranges, perhaps comparable to the Alps, have been stripped away, laying bare this nub. I begin to sense what has occurred here, the forces that have been at work, the explosions, the rumblings, the upheaval, the pressure, the heat intense enough to shoot streams of molten rocks hundreds of feet through fissures.

Diane Ettles

There's a Bible story about encouraging the weak of heart to enter the Holy of Holies, isn't there? That box canyon falls is a holy place. The water falls a great way with a very gentle sound, not like waterfalls generally. The falls are a long continuous bow of rock, quite smooth. The trees and ferns and lush green growth sigh gently in the downdrafts of warm breezes from the scorching red sun country above, but within the falls' basin all is quiet. The climbers bathed in the pool and in near-silence, drank in the sacred nature of the place. A holy of holies for a Sunday on the Colorado.
—FROM THE GROUP JOURNAL

Black Tail Canyon/Mile 120

Sue Hirschfield, geologist

I find myself going through the workday and suddenly a vision will flash through my mind—some great rock formation—a wave—or Dr. Sue's smile—and I think, What am I doing here—dressed like this—how tidy—I'm really much different!
                                —DIANE ETTLES

Joy Hardin

Later today, Sue comments on differences between her experiences on our women's trip and mixed trips. Here she feels that she can allow her feelings of fear and find the support she needs to go through them; here she is tested, but not judged.

Being in the paddle boat through the series of rapids yesterday had tremendous implications for her life, she tells me. She learned how effective it is to reach out with your paddle into the wave that threatens to engulf you. The danger comes in holding back, which actually escalates the chance of being knocked overboard. Though your initial reaction is to pull back, the safest response is to dig your paddle into the wave itself, creating a third point of balance. She recognizes how often the same principle is true in our lives, how holding back creates difficulties, can heighten danger rather than eliminate it.

Joy Hardin, an early member of Women in the Wilderness, joins us and also comments on the differences between women's trips and mixed trips. Joy has completed a doctoral dissertation on the subject of women and leadership and the outdoor experience at the University of Massachusetts. Her work grew out of her experience in women's courses all over the country, ranging from Outward Bound trips to overnights for black women on the shores of Lake Michigan in Chicago. She found more sharing of the leader's role and more disclosure of feelings in women's groups than in mixed groups. On women's trips, she noticed encouragement and support for women to choose their own goals and take risks. In mixed groups, she found women tend to take the traditional roles of cooking and cleaning, and support the generally male leadership. Women's trips, she concluded, force the nontraditional role of leader and explorer upon us, giving more room to grow.

Joy and I met some years ago when she was doing her field research. We became immediate and close friends, though her living in Massachusetts and my living in California posed a problem. In response, we decided that Women in the Wilderness had to have a national network, an eastern contingent as well as a western one. At the time the organization consisted of six of us in the West and Joy in the East, hardly a national network. It grew out of Joy's and my letters to each other, our phone calls and any excuse to get together. But the idea took root and Women in the Wilderness grew beyond its California boundaries. Her presence on this trip, her first white-water experience, is a special pleasure for me.

Later in the day while we're drifting on the river, someone suggests that we each take a turn telling the most frightening moments of our lives, our narrowest escapes. Joy recalls a slip while winter climbing. Louise, our chief guide, relates a story about a night she was sleeping on her boat not too far above Lava Falls. The boat was tied to a tree;

as the water level dropped overnight, the boat washed down the river, taking the tree with it. Clad only in her tennis shoes and a belt on which she carried her knife, she jumped to the rope that was dragging the tree, cut herself free, gave a shout, leaped to the one oar she could use, and rowed without stopping, pulling in to the opposite shore, just above the falls.

My own such moment came when I was carrying my three-year-old daughter piggyback across a large beaver dam at the confluence of several creeks in the Colorado mountains. I lost my balance and we fell in on the upstream side of the dam. We could easily have been pinned against the dam by the current and drowned, but because of the force of the several creeks that came together there was a large opening in the dam underwater and we washed through. Though we were loose in the mountain current, somehow, through maternal instinct, I grabbed her and held her face out of the water until we were rescued downstream.

Ironically, Katie Knopke, an Outward Bound instructor, experienced her uttermost fear indoors. Her moment came at the end of a love affair when she woke up in the middle of the night crying, tearing her bed sheets into tatters.

We float on, past shining black schists and gneiss formations, polished smooth by the river, curving silver in the afternoon sun. Four green-winged teal fly by low. A storm builds up in the distance, rapids rumble ahead. Upstream winds set in for the afternoon as we row on steadily against them. A black butterfly flutters around the boats, buffeted by the winds.

That night a storm erupts but it's not the weather. After dinner I am sitting in the boats with the guides when suddenly one of the women runs up along the beach screaming at the top of her lungs at us: "I paid my money for you to make me happy, and I'm not and it's all your fault. Get me out of here. I want a helicopter."

Here was a woman who had been talked into making the trip. I suppose she was suffering the consequences of not having made that decision for herself. Being with women only was a new and frightening experience for her, and the Canyon itself is an intense experience. Though I tried to talk with her, she refused to speak with me since I was "responsible" for her unhappiness in having organized the trip.

I am realizing that solitude is not aloneness or loneliness but strength in self. All else follows from that. I revel in the fact that this trip has provided me with my first real sense of self.

—CHERYL WEINER

The incident was laughable. Or was it? There was an element in the whole interaction that was more saddening than anything else. You can only avoid yourself for so long, particularly in a place like the Grand Canyon. Ultimately you run into the fact of yourself, stripped of your day-to-day context. I couldn't take her difficulties on myself; nor could I ignore them; I never knew what they were. So I am left to speculate and would guess that the intensity of the river, coupled with the fear

Stone Creek/Mile 132

It's corny, it's trite, I've read all the same kinds of accounts, and none of that matters. Today I fell out in a rapid and I am connected to these women and the river in a wholly new way. A baptism, China called it, and that sounded pretty close. A losing of fear, a plunge into trust, a transformation from unknown to the highly respected but akin. . . . Drawn as much by river as by these good riverwomen, I am in some new totalness of both trust and freedom.

—JOY HARDIN

that some women have of being alone with other women, created the outburst.

Everyone else remained pleasant, which took some effort. The trip was too important for the rest of us to let it be marred. She had been difficult all along; that seemed to be her style. And yet her childishness nagged at me. I saw myself, years ago, before it ever occurred to me that I was responsible for myself, or, as one friend put it, that life "is a do-it-yourself job." Until then, I had imagined that everyone else caused my difficulties, my predicaments, and my unhappiness. I imagined that I was innocent. Finally my life became so painful that whether someone else was the cause of my unhappiness or not was beside the point. I was willing to do whatever was necessary to change it.

The next morning at Stone Creek, I set out alone, wanting and needing time to myself. Like a child, I wade in the stream bed in the early-morning heat, caught in the creek's babble. The unpleasantness of the evening washes away. I am moved, in my element. The side canyon continues to widen as I hike deeper and deeper into its recesses. I find lizards and lime-green grasshoppers, and a mud dauber wasp nest. The sun is hot, cicadas drone, the creek is cool on my feet. I wade over pink granites, pebbles, and green mosses, keen to behold the place.

That night Joy and I sleep by the creek. The sadness of divorce continues to be with me off and on throughout the trip. Joy cheers me, bringing back my good spirits with her own. In the morning we wake early and I see that for a change she is the one troubled. Her face is expressive, her moods revealed. She has had nightmares and wakens sad, aware of the uprootedness of her own life. Finished with her research, she will move from the country into the city upon her return. A new work, a new place to live, all transitions that might have gone unremarked except for being here, where the Canyon makes them clear.

The desert which we hiked through yesterday now seems harsh to her, unmitigated in its intensity, its heat, its starkness. She lets herself sit and cry for a while; I hold her close. No explanation is needed. Sometimes sadness will break out, coursing like a river, seeking its own level, filling in empty places. No hesitation: emotional simplicity. The Canyon leaves few hiding places.

After breakfast, we hike up through sedimentary rocks which are riddled with the marks and abandoned burrows of tiny mud animals which lived millions of years ago. Such numbers are beyond my comprehension, but I can know the red of the rock bright in the desert sun, its rough surface, and see the tracings of another creature, clear and shaped by a particular way of life. Green, ocher, orange, and yellow lichens tell us that these rocks have not moved for hundreds of years. These markings are all we can know.

DAY 11

We leave the river for a day, hiking four miles south up Havasu Creek
to spend the afternoon at Beaver Falls. The creek runs down the dozen
or so miles between the Havasu Indian Reservation and the Colorado
River, spilling over travertine waterfalls, one after another, which range
from two hundred feet to six inches in height. Between the falls are
swollen aquamarine pools spilling down the long side canyon, lush with
wild grapevines.

I stop to watch an assembly of brown butterflies flutter over a bloom-
burdened tree beside the creek. Time stops and for a moment tree and
butterflies merge in graceful tremulousness, the air a constant motion
of brown wings edged in light. The incessant opening and closing of
wings, butterflies lighting and landing, hovering, delineate a country
of the air. I am tangled in their movements. I give over to this slow
motion and finally am reminded of my own. After an age of
consideration, I break away and continue up the creek to Beaver Falls.

The hike to Beaver Falls is filled with green mosses, red monkey
flowers, travertine rock, great cottonwoods, manzanita, ocotillo cactus,
maidenhair ferns breaking out of rocks, and the constant nag of grapevine
at my legs. Underneath a fifty-foot cascade at Beaver Falls is a cave
that you have to swim across the creek to enter. Louise mentioned it
to Suzanne this morning as she packed her wet suit before we began
the hike. Butterflies, blue dragonflies, canyon wrens calling, the sigh
of cicadas, creation breathing while the water is falling, tumbling over
a cave we cannot see but only hear of. I am afraid of caves, of being
trapped, of having no air. I have been in a cave only once before. Like
moths to flames, we are drawn to our deepest fears. The dilemma is
the transformation, entering into the place of our terror. I am burning
by the time I arrive and find Louise standing by the creek with Suzanne,
laughing, saying, "China, we found it, the cave . . . you've got to go
in, you'll love it."

I can see Louise's excitement and would feel safe with her. I agree
to go if she will lead us. She refuses, saying that Joy and I should do
it together. Her leading us would ruin the pleasure of our finding our
own way.

"It's easy," Louise exclaims. "You'll have no trouble."

Joy says, "Look, China, I've done a lot of caving back East and that
part doesn't scare me as much as having to swim underwater and come
out underneath a waterfall. And that part doesn't scare you as much
as it does me. We have complementary fears. We can do it." With mixed
feelings I agree.

Louise gives us her diving mask and we dive in, swimming hard
diagonally against the swift current to reach the other side. We find a
rock ledge and climb out near the other side of the waterfall. Louise

and Suzanne stand on the other side watching us. The noise of the falls drowns out any communication except by waving arms. Joy slips into the water, still holding on to the rock ledge, and begins to inch her way toward an opening that may be the entrance. Suzanne and Louise gesticulate wildly from the other shore, waving their hands, shaking their heads no, yelling, but we can't hear them. I shout to Joy that she's going into the wrong place and wonder what might be the consequences of such a mistake. An error at this point would not be visible. We would simply not return.

Joy moves slightly left. Suzanne and Louise gesture approvingly. There is an opening, an empty space perhaps three feet wide and ten inches high in the rock just above the surface of the water. Joy ducks down, going underneath the rock overhead to investigate. She has found it. We're at the entrance. "This is it. There's plenty of room in here," she shouts back to me. "I'll come in this first part," I tell her, "but I don't know if I'll go any further."

As I climb up beside her in the first chamber underneath the waterfall it's very dark, the only light is reflected from the thin band of an opening we just came through. To my surprise, I discover there is enough space for four people to sit comfortably, but it's dark, cold, slippery. The falls roar as we move in closer to the center of the rock formation that the water pours over. "Joy, I don't think I'm going any further." Patient, she assures me that whatever I do is fine. She begins exploring the walls of the cave, feeling for the small hole beside a log Louise described as the entrance to the underwater tunnel to the next chamber. Moving slowly along the walls in the dim light she says, "I think I've found it, here, come feel this, China." I reached down with my hand along the rough cold rock. Yes, there is an opening to be felt underwater. No light, felt but not seen. Relying on the unfamiliar sense of touch, I stick my hand into an opening. Louise has told us that we can put a leg through and feel air on our feet on the other side once we are completely submerged in the tunnel. But first we have to be submerged. This is the hard part: hearing that something is possible and doing it yourself are wildly different. There was Louise, dark-haired, laughing, only moments ago, saying that what is before me is possible, probable. Yet the next chamber looms in a distance that is beyond my reckoning. Again I tell Joy that I may turn back. Again she says, "Fine." She will move ahead slowly and assures me that I can follow if I feel so inclined. And then she is coming up on the other side, in the next chamber, shouting, "It's fine! Come ahead, there's plenty of room and plenty of air." Her words come floating through, blurred in the passage of sound through water. I reply, "I'm not sure I can do this," while I'm putting first one leg into the hole, then the other, surprised at all the room; now my hips, now the moment when suddenly I realize that, despite my reluctance, I am going. "Here I come," I shout and go under, feet first into the darkness, underwater, moving through the tunnel, on my back with my hands pushing myself through, breech-style, and I am in a chamber, smaller than the first, sitting next to Joy. Now I laugh at my fears. Ahead of us is another low passage and the light from the final chamber.

The light comes up bright after the darkness as we crawl on our bellies through the passage into the last room. Emerging, we are startled by the beauty of this place, so spacious and airy and bathed in blue light. The waterfall is loudest now that we are directly underneath it. We sit in the silence of all this sound. Inside the light we are twenty thousand leagues under the sea, we are inside the belly of the whale, we are on an ocean shelf. For a moment, we are ancient and wise. I sit Indian fashion, taking it all in, blue light, the cold, wet joy of discovery, the unmoving air, rock walls, the deepening friendship. We have found the place . . .

> Where we meet our outcast selves. . . . Where we go into darkness. Where we embrace darkness. Where we lie close to darkness, breathe when darkness breathes and find darkness inside ourselves. . . . Where we are not afraid, Where joy is just under the surface.
> The shape of a cave, we say, or the shape of a labyrinth. The way we came here was dark. Space seemed to close in on us. We thought we could not move forward. We had to shed our clothes. We had to leave all we brought with us. And when we finally moved through this narrowing opening, our feet reached for ledges, under was an abyss. . . . Our voices echoed off the walls. . . .
> The shape of this cave, our bodies, this darkness.
> The shape of a cave, this emptiness we seek out like water . . . Drawn by the one who came before. And before her. And before. Back to the beginning. To the one who first swam from the mouth of this cave.
> This round cavern, motion turned back on itself, the follower becomes the followed, moon in the sky, the edge becomes the center, what is buried emerges, light dying over the water, what is unearthed is stunning, the we we're seeking, turning with the ways of this earth, is ourselves.
> . . . The shape of our silence, the shape of the roofs of our mouths. Darkness.
> —Susan Griffin, *Woman and Nature*

Darkness to blue light. Why is the light blue in the deepest part, turquoise, azure, manganese blue? Every shade escapes the color, the blue you must find for yourself. I am only a sculptor molding, finding the shape of my being in this canyon, among these rocks, sharp, now smooth, cold-wet, dry-hot, moss-covered, lichened, ferned, burned.

We are exultant, reveling in the light, yet soon we must leave, Joy tells me. She is getting chilled. In the heat of my excitement I fail to notice the cold, but she is right. We have only thin bathing suits, no wet suits or means of retaining our body warmth. Though the creek is not as cold as the Colorado River, it is only two to three degrees warmer.

The obvious way out is underneath the large ledge, the underwater entrance to the cave, from which all the light is coming. That means a dive of six feet or so down to the entrance and then out underwater into what we cannot see. How long will we have to stay underwater? There's no way to tell at this point. Now Joy begins to talk of going back out the way we came in. We exchange roles. This plunge is the most fearful part for her. Our being directly under the falls means diving deep into the place where all the water is pouring down. There is an eddy behind the falls. Will we be caught?

Yet I feel confident that the exit must be simple and offer to dive down and look with the diving mask. Even with the mask, all I can see is a storm of bubbles underwater at the opening, and the creek bottom, boned clean from the enormous pressure of water cutting into it. I surface and tell her that this must be the way out and offer to go first. "I'll wait below at the entrance. Grab onto my ankle and I'll lead the way." Reassured now by me as I had been by her, Joy agrees to come with me rather than threading her way back through the tunnels. We dive down underneath the ledge; she grabs my ankle, we pause and push out into the turbulence underneath. Instantly we are torn apart and tossed up separately to the surface. I come up downstream in the fast current. Joy surfaces where she had feared, in the eddy behind the falls, but is soon sucked under again and spit out downstream. We've done it! We swim hard to shore, excited, ecstatic. Suzanne and Louise have been waiting to greet us, and for a moment we all laugh and howl at the dark, at our fears, trembling with the excitement of finding the cave.

When I said to a stranger at church one day after a sermon on the people following Moses into the wilderness: "What does 'women in the wilderness' sound like to you?" And he said, "Women who are lost and searching." No way were we lost! Not for a moment. We are women who are challenged and who are growing stronger day by day.

—LAREE ZIERK

Lava Falls/Mile 180

DAY 12

The tension this morning is like a wired fence sparking at the slightest touch. Today we run Lava Falls. Water flow is about fifteen hundred cubic feet per second, giving Lava a solid ten rating on the scale of difficulty for rapids. Number ten. Lava marks the outer limit.

Our plan for running it is to set ourselves up for the "slot," a narrow section of water that shoots straight through the falls and gives us our only chance of avoiding major obstacles. The slot is only three feet in the midst of a churning hundred-foot-wide expanse of falling water. We have only seconds to make our move; a foot off on either side in that fast current means that we miss and all hell breaks loose.

Only six of us will paddle through Lava. Barb Dupuis, our paddle-boat captain, thinks the only fair way to select our crew is to draw

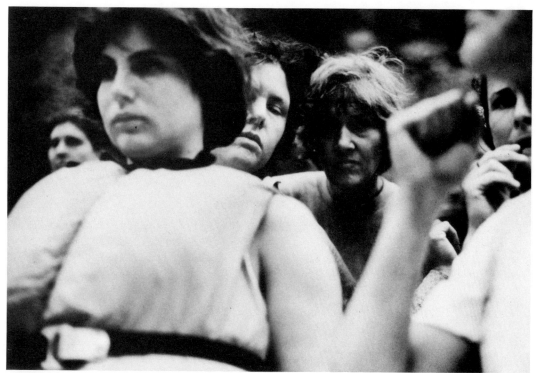

Paddle-boat crew: Looking over Lava Falls

straws. We settle for twigs, breaking six off short as a sign of being a crew member. At least ten of us want to paddle. Though our chances of flipping the boat are high—fifty-fifty—my preference is to paddle, knowing that at least I'll be thrown clean, no "death lines" or gear to get tangled in, to trap me in a rapid underneath a capsized boat.

"Death lines" are loose long ends of the webbing used to tie the boat loads down. If a boat flips and a piece of webbing wraps around you underneath the boat it can easily become a "death line." When we tie the loads down this morning, we help with all possibilities in mind, checking carefully to see that all gear is secured and no webbing is left loose. The mist that covers much of our day-to-day life is burned off in the heat of the apparent risks we are taking. The possibility of death is no longer veiled or mere morbid consideration; it is valid and essential to take into account.

If we make the slot, Barb will yell the command "Drop!" as we go into the first enormous wave. Then we'll automatically pop back up, released from the pressure of thousands of gallons of water pouring over us, and paddle like fury until the rapid ends. We agree and quietly position ourselves in the raft.

We pull out into the current, back paddling to position ourselves before being swept over the falls. Though my heart is pounding, my breath is steady. We are poised, ready to spring. We drift closer. From the back of the raft where she is standing, directing our strokes, Barb yells "Drop!" and we hit the floor, keeping the weight low and central. I'm in the back next to Barb to help rudder as we make our dive. The front of the raft comes up and a solid wall of gray water comes pouring down on us from overhead. It feels as if we're capsizing end over end. I can't tell if I'm in the boat or out of it, and then in a split second I know that I'm out as the next twenty-five-foot wave engulfs me, plunging me beneath the surface.

I begin to panic but realize that I'm only wasting time. All there is to do is breathe whenever possible and relax in the middle of this intense turbulence. Nothing more. Nothing less. Time balloons, full and swollen; seconds expand into minutes; there is only the gray thundering water, the constant boiling, and my presence of mind. I look over my right shoulder and see an immense wave that will take me under again. I take a deep breath and give over to the forces of a wild river, an explosion of water. Twenty-five feet over my head, the wave tip curls, breaks, and crashes down on me, pummeling me into the vortex of the turbulence itself. Down, around, until the next moment, tossed up like a twig to the surface again. I am through the rapid. It has all happened within forty-five seconds.

I look around and see that the paddle boat has not capsized and is just upstream of me, midriver, close enough for me to swim to. Somehow I still have my paddle in my hand. Someone grabs it, pulling me to the boat, then grabs me by the seat of my pants, frantically catapulting me back into the raft. I'm safe. So is Barb, who washed out with me. They have pulled her back in just before me. We give a shout. We're all accounted for and the boat has not flipped.

Barb quickly assumes command again and orders us to bail with a frenzy. The boat is filled to the brim with water and is barely maneuverable. We have to pull into an eddy and empty it so that we aren't swept into the next rapid downstream uncontrolled. More important, we are the rescue boat for the last snout rig, which is just beginning to make its run. By the time we're able to pull into the eddy, they've made a beautiful run and have no need of us. We can relax. We pull to shore and turn the boat over, emptying hundreds of gallons of water back into the river.

I am left stripped, vulnerable, and bare. I feel transparent, like a child, unable to disguise my feelings. The pounding of my heart vibrates throughout my entire body. I am safe, there are friends holding me, laughing. I shake my head as though waking from a dream and let out a loud "whoopeeee!"

The cabin where I write faces west, looks out toward the sea cliffs. Morning's fire burns at my back in the wood stove. The rain hurls itself against the glass in front of me and mottles my view of the world. The rain pours down, winds whip round the corners under the doors, bending all the trees, which dance on the wall of glass in front of me.

Soon I leave for Baja, ocean kayaking in the Sea of Cortez.

—CHINA GALLAND

II   The Nature of the Seabed

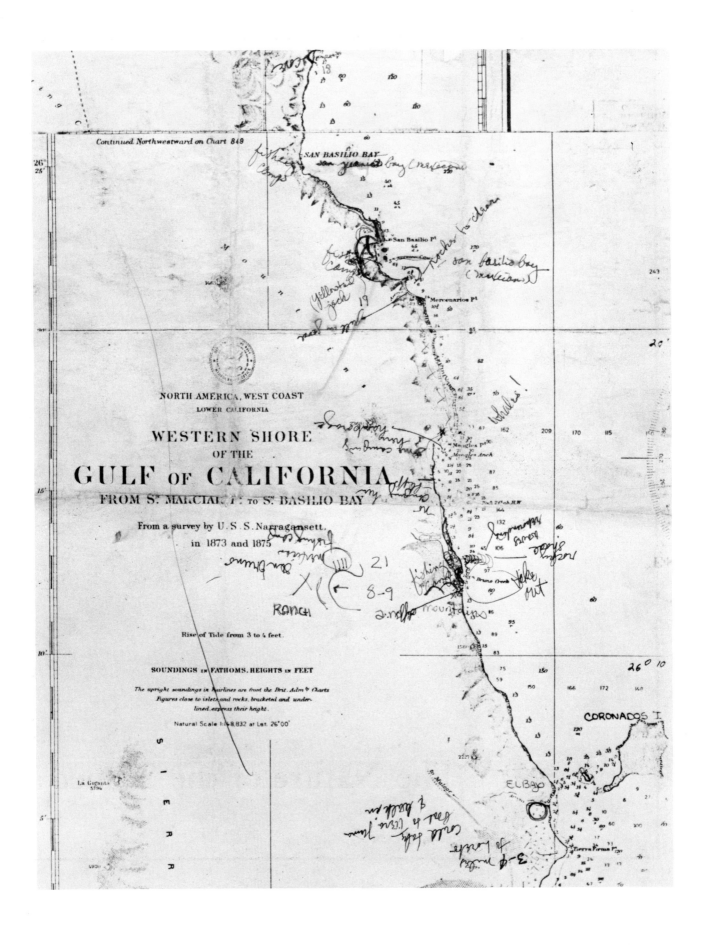

Continued Northwestward on Chart 849

SAN BASILIO BAY

San Basilio Pt

Mercenarios Pt

NORTH AMERICA, WEST COAST

LOWER CALIFORNIA

WESTERN SHORE
OF THE
GULF OF CALIFORNIA
FROM St. MARCIAL Pt. TO St. BASILIO BAY

From a survey by U.S.S. Narragansett.
in 1873 and 1875

Rise of Tide from 3 to 4 feet.

SOUNDINGS IN FATHOMS. HEIGHTS IN FEET

The upright soundings in hairlines are from the Brit. Adm.y Charts
Figures close to islets and rocks, bracketed and under-
lined express their height.

Natural Scale 1 in 8,832 at Lat. 26°00'

SIERRA

La Giganta
5794

CORONADOS I.

EL BAJO

II

The Nature of the Seabed
*all-women's ocean kayaking expedition,
Baja, Mexico*

*Not to have known either the mountain
or the desert is not to have known one's
self. Not to have known oneself is to have
known no one.*
—JOSEPH WOOD KRUTCH,
Baja, The Geography of Hope

aja, Mexico, the Sea of Cortez. I put together a nineteen-day
ocean-kayaking school for Women in the Wilderness with
National Outdoor Leadership School (NOLS).

EVENING, MARCH 1
Los Angeles airport. My notes begin as I write last-minute letters;
loudspeakers blare, paging a different person each time.

MARCH 2
Midmorning, flight from Los Angeles to Mulegé, halfway down the
Baja peninsula. We fly over mountains, sand-sculpted deserts, salt lakes,
rectangles of irrigated green contrasting with the desert that this land
is always reverting to. On my right is the Sea of Cortez. To the left
are fluted dunes, shaped by the winds blowing from the sea.

Lucie Smith, one of our instructors from the National Outdoor
Leadership School, sits next to me on the plane. Tall, lanky, bandana-
shirted, wearing stitched black western boots, she has sandy hair and
keen blue eyes. She lives in Wyoming, chews Copenhagen, and sings
Spanish love songs and rugby ditties with full British accent. We talk
briefly, sharing our appreciation of the inhabitants of the smaller
Mexican villages. I like her instinctively.

Lucie leans over to point out Isla Carmen, where the bodies were
found of two of the three people who drowned last spring on the route
we will take. The mountains are drenched in the day's last light. We
land in Mulegé at a small airstrip adjacent to our hotel, the Serenidad.

We sleep by a river that runs to the sea.

MARCH 3

At seven in the morning, the sun is rising, casting long shadows across the red-tiled porches at the Serenidad.

We meet Abby Caul, our head instructor, in the lobby of the hotel. Though only in her mid-twenties, Abby has already spent three seasons in Baja and is quite experienced. Her warm brown eyes and confident manner put everyone at ease.

We sit by a fire and talk briefly about our plans, then pile into a blue pickup with our gear and head south twenty miles to the NOLS headquarters at Coyote Bay. There we spend the morning sorting through personal gear, repacking, paring our baggage down to essentials. For three weeks we will travel down the coast by kayak, fishing and learning basic survival and leadership skills as we do. We are issued diving weights, spear guns, fishing rods, hand slings, life jackets, and books on the environment.

Abby distributes copies of the most accurate map of the area; it was made in 1873. We are in Baja, Mexico, and hardly any maps are available. Abby has used this one for years and knows its accuracies and inaccuracies. It will suffice, she assures us with a smile. The pace is leisurely, giving enough time to sort, pack, and check our gear; to make sure that our wet suits fit. Tonight we sleep on the beach.

MARCH 4

We waken in the dark at four-thirty in the morning and begin to load the boats. Our expedition is self-contained; we carry all our supplies for the nineteen days. Our dive bags contain wet suits, masks, fins, and thirty pounds of lead weight. In addition we have bags of dry food, forty-pound water jugs, and personal gear, all of which must be completely loaded and unloaded from our boats each day. Each night we will carry the eighty-pound boats up onto the beach.

Our vessels, folboats, are two-person, oceangoing kayaks. We carry them down to the beach this morning and load them standing knee high in the cold surf.

Abby begins the course with a discussion of the weather. Deceptively benign, it can change with a speed that creates the greatest danger for the traveler here. Our first lesson is learning to read the wind. This morning it's from the west, and with calm water, which indicates that it's safe to travel, she explains. The northeast wind is the one that brings danger in the Sea of Cortez, sweeping down over two hundred miles of open sea. It can build up heavy, rolling surf and whitecaps within ten minutes, tossing canvas-skinned folboats around like loose change, capsizing or breaking them up on the rocks. This is what happened to the three people who drowned last spring.

One of the most important elements of this trip is the chance to

Assembling a folboat

develop and examine leadership abilities. This NOLS course is based on the assumption that leadership is primarily a skill, one that can be learned and transmitted, that each of us is a leader and can function as such in a group, given certain skills and understanding. We will take turns, rotating leadership among ourselves each day.

Upon waking, the leader of the day is responsible for checking the wind. If it's blowing hard from the northeast, she'll tell everyone to go back to sleep; we'll stay in camp. But, more often, the wind is from another direction or is shifting. Whether or not we get out on the water in the morning is the crucial decision. Some expeditions have been stranded for days by high winds. People have drowned from poor judgment or lack of respect. Check the wind, learn to read the weather. This first week we'll all climb in the dark to some unobstructed spot with our instructors to check the wind. After that we have to make our own decisions without them.

During the day Lucie and Abby often mention a small-group expedition. We don't understand the term. Then they explain that for the last three days of our nineteen-day course we will travel without them and without any food except what we can catch ourselves.

The response to this is mixed. Sheila had arrived from the East Coast thinking that the entire course would be run without any food except what we could catch. Sally resents the news. It's more than she bargained for. The same is true for Robin. Marilyn is game and so am I. Providing for ourselves makes explicit another dimension of this journey for me. But at the same time I understand full well the hard feelings about NOLS created by withholding this information prior to departure. Now there are no options. I would have preferred it otherwise. This is traditional leadership, which assumes that people do not need to be informed or have options. Someone else, the leader, knows best. Geared toward efficiency, it runs the danger of creating friction.

New-style leadership assumes that people are basically responsible and make good decisions when fully informed. Cooperation can arise more easily when everyone has the opportunity to make her own decisions. But we are here now. We choose to go on with the course. The instructions take on more importance. When the time comes, we will select a leader from our own group, traveling by ourselves the final twenty-five miles of coastline to our takeout point at San Bruno, one hundred miles away.

We all want to be fully informed of what we've signed up for, yet I've rarely seen this happen on wilderness trips. The experience itself is so different from anything that can be described as you sit comfortably at home. Deep down the choice to go into the wilderness is also a longing to let go and a willingness to take life on whatever terms it offers; yet we are fearful of that letting-go and resist it.

The idea of eating only what food we can catch or collect makes sense to me. People have always lived this way and may have to again. I can imagine a day when the only food available is the food I catch, when I must know the ways of the weather because my safety and that of my family and companions is at stake. Do I long for that day? Do our bones remember, our hands remember? Our body remembers, though the mind forgets, what it is to know our surroundings so well, to depend on them so entirely, that we are part of them—not separate from this coast, these plants, these birds and fish. The Greek poet George Seferis says the trees are seaweed and we are but fish swimming in bright air. I want to know how to feed myself.

Frigate birds wheel slowly overhead. As I paddle this morning I realize that I don't know why I am here. I have many reasons, but no answer. It is enough to be here.

We see brown-footed boobies, osprey, pelicans, oystercatchers.

MARCH 5

The wind is strong from the north. We put off our crossing of Bahía Concepción for the day, remaining in camp and learning first aid in the field. We cover bleeding, breathing, and shock. We are told that hearing is the last sense to go. We learn about cardiopulmonary resuscitation and enact an emergency. We take turns simulating CPR, which combines pumping the chest, to stimulate the heart, with mouth-to-mouth breathing. Count the breaths: one, two, three, four, five, and PUMP, one, two, three, four, five, PUMP, one, two, and the sun's hot and PUMP one and is she alive and PUMP one and two and three and PUMP no room for error, you dare PUMP not miss a breath a count PUMP or you can lose someone's life PUMP I hold it in my hands, PUMP in my breath out and in breathing PUMP deep the heart to start, PUMP breathe, PUMP and breathe. You have to stay PUMP with them, it can be for PUMP hours, and you breathe for them PUMP until you are exhausted and PUMP.

This is life, it could be your life. We are told not to start CPR unless we are prepared to stay with it to the end, the end being life or death. I imagine that I would want to start rather than have to live with the question "what if?" Some people go crazy with regret.

This is the dark side of the moon. For all the beauty of a journey into the wilderness, injury and death are its terrors. Someone may be injured, someone you don't even know or like, and it's up to you to help, only because you happened to be there. You don't like it, you don't think you deserve this set of circumstances, no one ever told you what to do, you'd rather be anywhere but here, with this person, injured and unconscious and there is no time left. There is only the choice: yes or no. Choose to stay and you'll have to do everything you can imagine, remember, or conjure up as you attempt to save a life. Or you can say no, turn your back, and walk away with the question "Could I have helped?" Could I have made a difference even in my ignorance?

We go over maps and compasses, directions, all of which are useless unless you already know where you are. You have to be able to locate yourself in order to use a map. I remember that I have no map of my own; I am making a rutter. I am in the process of locating myself, discovering the nature of the seabed and making notes, voluminous notes. I am learning to distinguish the edible plants from the poisonous, to hunt, to fish, to feed myself.

Inevitably comes the killing. Where does it stop? Why kill one form of life and not another? Because fish don't scream, can we assume there is no pain as they lie gasping for air, a fillet knife cutting them up from the anus, then a slice down the back, parting the skin from the meat. And this is what I'm here for. There is a certain kind of knowledge that we hide from. Let someone else do the killing, the packaging; give the victim another name. Call the pig pork; the cow beef. Leave me out of this, remove it from my sight, my hook, my knife, my hand. I am innocent—no more.

We break after three hours and draw maps of our lives. I pass out crayons and a long sheet of paper for each person. "How long is your life?" I ask. "Draw it like this coastline here in Baja, in colors that feel familiar. Where are the crossings you have to make? Where is the shore rocky, impossible to land on? Where are the long sandy stretches of beach? Are there islands off your coast?" At first some are reluctant,

If you came this way,
Taking any route, starting from
* anywhere,*
At any time or at any season,
It would always be the same . . .
    —T. S. ELIOT,
    "Little Gidding,"
    Four Quartets

Santa Domingo

Punta Colorado

but after going off for an hour alone with maps they return, wanting to show them and see the others.

Cryptic, colorful, each map is wildly different. We begin to get more of a sense of each other. Sally, who is fifty-five, studied anthropology while she was a rural social worker in northern California during the forties. She loved the outdoors. In those days, she was forbidden to camp out by her superiors because it was "unprofessional" to sleep out by night and see clients by day. Marilyn, twenty-six, is the middle child among ten children of Chinese immigrant parents who spoke no English. She grew up in a black neighborhood in San Francisco. She continually surprises me. Two days ago when we first began to snorkel, she was panicky. Now she is the first one in and is becoming a good fisher.

Generally on a NOLS course, instructors and students cook separately, but Robin voices the discomfort we all feel about this, and in the evening, as we begin to cook dinner in one group, the old distinctions between "student" and "instructor" begin to fade. The trip comes alive for me.

We set out in our folboats at first light just before sunrise; a school of porpoises play in front of us as we paddle across the bay, moving deeper into the natural world. Our crossing takes us to the largely uninhabited stretch of Baja. Moving further away from civilization, I feel more energetic, excited by the desert and sea around me.

Each day brings a new lesson. This morning we learn to snorkel and surf cast. We camp in an arroyo at Santo Domingo, a tiny deserted fishing village. A Mexican fishing boat, a panga, motors by, full of cursing gringos, their voices carried high and clear on the wind.

Later, as we paddle around the point, I am reminded of how foolish we are to judge one another. I struggle to keep the boat headed right as Shelia takes a stroke that throws my paddling off every time. With great effort and a lot of communication we learn to paddle together. There is no right and wrong; we have different rhythms, different styles of paddling. Some people are easy to paddle with, others require effort. But when you're working together the results are clear: the boat moves forward rapidly. This only happens by working together, by focusing on integration not differences.

MARCH 8

Notes from a sleepless night: I sleep on the beach and waken with the commotion of pelicans, diving and feeding in the night, splashing down for fish, then whoosh, beating the wind with their great wings and taking off only to dive again. The water is covered with the sparks of phosphorescence, which light each time the surface breaks. A pelican dives, a fish breaks the surface, and there is a small explosion of light. I can hear a whale breathe nearby; there she blows again. The wings

Trolling in the early morning

Water is the palace of the true dragon.

—DOGEN,
*Mountains and
River Sutra*

beat the air, a dive and a splash, blue white, electric: three pelicans hit the water in succession; the phosphorescence sparkles and ripples the dark. The moon comes out from behind the clouds. The sea, the birds are flashing in the night.

MARCH 9

Sunrise stretches thin and salmon across the sky. A whale blows, still nearby. Pinks melt into a hot glow of orange, red, and gold as the sun climbs, burning a hole into the sky. I turn over in my sleeping bag, happy in the growing understanding of the time that I require alone outdoors to balance my domestic life. Suddenly I begin to worry about my children, Matthew (fifteen), Madelon (fourteen), and Benjamin (ten). This separation is a test for us all. I have never left them for so long, and I begin to realize that much of what I'm enjoying on this trip I can do at home, with my family. And yet I have the compulsion to leave home in order to return. I require being left alone. Society may hold that the good mother is always at home and loving it, but I need some time away. I go into the wilderness and rediscover the home within. Learning my way around the wilds fills out and heightens my feelings for my family. There is a keenness that is honed by separation, an appreciation for others that surfaces out of these times away.

We see torote, elephant tree, leather plant, copal, ocotillo, cholla, cardon, pataya dulce, pataya agria, palo verde.

Later in the day, Abby takes us on a walk and points out the different cactuses and desert bushes. Several of the plants we see cannot be identified; there is no definitive plant book on Baja. The existing ones are spotty and incomplete. How good it is to be in a place so remote that not everything is known, identified. The maps are old and incomplete, the plants defy classification. The more I learn the less I know; after I identify one plant's name and habitat, there are three more beside it which escape naming.

Ramorita

MARCH 13

Sally and I walk up an arroyo, identifying plants, trees, cactuses, wildflowers. Lucie and Robin, who's become an excellent fisherwoman, spear a red snapper and a shark. I go off alone to sit zazen, the Zen Buddhist form of meditation. Lucie bakes fresh bread and brownies in the heat of the day. After I come back, I sit to the side and just watch everyone. In an improvised shower, Shelia pours salt water over Robin, whose naked body glistens in the afternoon sun.

I am surprised by other people's willingness to participate in whatever is at hand; I find myself withdrawing from the constant group activity, understanding more my growing need for solitude, to be alone. This is what I need to balance the intense and constant activity of my family life.

The midafternoon desert heat makes the air above the rocks shimmer and wave. Vision: The sea alters perspective, plays tricks with focus. From here Isla Ildefonso looks close, but is thirteen miles away at sea. Pulpito, an extinct volcano, looks much farther in the distance, but is only five miles away. When we dive with our masks the world is magnified. When I see the waves break underwater, the reefs are transformed and become brief bursts of light.

Two hours later the small shark Lucie speared is still alive. "They die hard," she explains.

MARCH 15

In a few days we will put out on our small-group expedition and I am apprehensive, still uncomfortable with the scale of our map, having misread it so often. It delineates some stretches of the coast accurately but is misleading on others. Some large coves are simply omitted. It is hard to distinguish between a rock and an island; bays are misnamed. Yet once we embark on the water we are committed: there are several stretches of coast where sheer cliffs jut out of the water, offering no place to land for miles. Abby and Lucie explain that there can be moments when it is safer to remain on the water in swelling seas and high winds than to attempt to land in the surf, crashing onto the rocks. Once again, experience is the only reliable guide. Because Abby has traveled this coast several times, she is able to correct the map, to draw in coves and bays which are not shown, to point out the Mexican fishing camps that are here. The map itself is not enough. We need a rutter. The seabed changes.

Briefly we discuss the pinnipeds: the seals, walruses, and sea lions. We paddled past many of these creatures this morning. They are still attached to the land for their mating and whelping and they retreat to the land for safety. Evolution. We were once sea creatures, who have now taken to the land. Whales were first sea, then land creatures, and now are sea creatures again. Seals, walruses, and sea lions likewise were land creatures, then sea creatures, and now live on both land and sea. How could this transformation have taken place? I speed up the evolutionary process in my mind and see a cow standing near the water's edge, growing as though it's being pumped up like a balloon. Fins burst from its sides, the head grows enormous, the breadth of several cars extends between its eyes, and as it grows it falls into the water, leaving only a giant fan, once its swishing tail, on shore.

San Nicolás

MARCH 16

We set out early, walking two miles south from our camp at Ramorita to the fishing village of San Nicolás, a settlement of five Mexican families. The desert is in full bloom from early winter rain. I am glad to have my paints and stop whenever possible to do a quick watercolor. We find date palms near the village that were planted hundreds of years ago by Jesuit missionaries. The arroyo leading to the village is thick with white prickly poppy and jimson weed blossoms. The village consists

of a few head of cattle, some goats, a handful of families, and long gardens of onions, peppers, tomatoes, and beans. Here we will spend the day resupplying ourselves with food and water. Visitors are few along this coast, and so Chico and Francesca, who welcome us here, make a celebration of our arrival, turning it into a warm social event.

Chico has barbecued a goat in our honor, and provides a little beer and tequila. Francesca and Honoraria lay the tables with big blue enamel pots steaming hot, full of beans, goat stew, barbequed ribs, and cole slaw. We eat together along with another group from NOLS, while in the background Mexican music plays on the tape deck in Chico's truck.

After lunch we talk in broken Spanish with Chico and make tortillas with Honoraria. The flies and chickens take over the table. Jokingly, Chico asks me if I would be a wife to Monty, the American who lives in the village half the year. Monty drinks too much sometimes and drives off the desert roads, a behavior that Chico thinks a wife would put an end to. We all laugh and pass around the tequila. "No, gracias."

MARCH 17   Santa Antonita

Turista strikes and Sheila grows ill, weakened by the nausea, and yet we have a hard stretch of paddling to do. We begin earlier than usual, waking at three-forty-five in the morning by the light of the full moon. We have decided to be on the water by five-thirty since today is the day we plan to cross over the Pulpito. This is the most dangerous crossing we will have to make on the entire journey. Here is where the three people drowned last March.

After dinner last night we discussed our plans and I insisted on an early crossing. Now I am unwilling to listen to complaints about rising so early or the suggestion that we save time by skipping breakfast. We need our strength. What small discomfort is worth a life? We say that people have accidents but sometimes we die out of sheer laziness. The natural world demands an alertness that civilization has lost. We have to be able to sleep deeply, dream, and waken fully. Simple. But, for the most part, we rest poorly, neglect our dreams, and walk about half asleep.

By the time we get up this morning there is no question that we are fully awake. We eat quietly and break camp more rapidly than usual. The full moon and Venus furnish us with light as we walk carefully over the rocky beach, hauling our boats down to the sea for loading. The sun won't rise for almost an hour, and we set out in the moonlit cold. I am glad to have Robin as my boat partner. We work well together and I enjoy her singing and her sense of humor. And she is strong.

Paddling this stretch of water we are completely exposed to the northeast, the most vulnerable position we can be in. Pulpito's sheer

straight walls rise hundreds of feet out of the water and can be seen
for miles. Just before Pulpito there is a bay at Santa Antonita in which
we can take shelter. But for these four miles before the bay there is
no safe place to pull in to shore. If the wind comes up, we have no
choice but to try to make the four miles. We paddle on in the darkness,
intent on making good time. As the sun begins to rise, the wind comes
up. Shortly thereafter, the sea begins to build into big swells. Paddling
across them grows tiring but we have no choice. Some of us are already
weakened with the turista, and we grow silent, focusing all our energies
on the work of keeping our small boats balanced in the swelling sea.
We paddle on across the wind, losing track of time. By eight we have
been paddling for three hours hard and steady with no break, and the
northeast wind seems to blow us back for every forward stroke we
take. The morning is bright, but the waves are whitecapping before
we can round Santa Antonita and the clouds streak across the sky. We
pull past a seal rookery at Santa Antonita, where our appearance has
set up a row. Waves are crashing. We have to make a decision quickly.
Robin is the leader for the day. We shout for the other boats to gather
as best they can in the noisy surf. Will we pull in here for the day or
try to make the run around Pulpito? It seems foolish. As we turn the
boats toward shore we are able to stop paddling across the swells for
a moment. Quickly the sea makes the choice as the swells lift our boats
and shoot us down the waves as though we were racing down a trough.
We laugh; the answer is obvious and we begin to pull for shore.

Pulpito

At our campsite later in the afternoon turista spreads; Abby grows
ill. That evening we talk more about leadership. Lucie has absorbed
the NOLS traditional style of giving instruction, while Abby is open
to shared decision making and discussion. We talk about the different
approaches. This is a group of adult women; we are in our late thirties
and mid-fifties with minds of our own. The tendency of the group is
to push for more self-determination and not necessarily along the lines
of NOLS' set curriculum. Robin expresses the difference clearly in her
willingness to spend time paddling to different possible campsites until
we have general agreement, rather than accepting an instructor's word
for which site to choose. This takes more time, but satisfies everyone.

I have often assumed that women's style of leadership differs markedly
from men's. But with this course I see that the attitudes vary and are
mixed between men and women. Too facile an assumption: as with
the rest of human life, the issue is more complex. Lucie's style is what
I might have called masculine in the past. But the terms are limited,
confusing to apply. The traditional style is hierarchical. The new style
is more horizontal, involving more participation in decision making.
The different ways of human organization around a task are many.
One style assumes that we are all capable of being leaders and that

the process is an interior one. The other assumes that only a few have the particular abilities necessary for leadership and therefore should have control over a group who will follow their intructions. Traditional leadership can be dangerous in this regard. This course gives me a chance to see how strongly I believe that we can all lead.

The need for the traditional style becomes clear only in the case of emergencies. Then one skilled person must be clearly in charge and instructions followed precisely and without question. At other times it's simply easier, but not necessary, to have one person in charge. Allowing people to arrive at their own decisions is essential to developing self-reliance. Abby seems to understand how for women this can be a particularly important aspect of a wilderness trip. We hash this over, talking late into the night.

MARCH 18

Pulpito

The weather is calm and we set out to round Pulpito at last. The water is glassy smooth and we are able to stay close to Pulpito's cliffs and see the seal rookery at the base. As we paddle past, thirty sea lions bark at us, setting up a row. Then one by one as we get closer, plop, they dive deep out of our sight. We round Pulpito with ease and set our course for Gull Rock, our last camp with our instructors before our final expedition.

Upon our arrival, the turista hits again. This time Sally and Robin take to their sleeping bags immediately upon making camp. My stomach is queasy too but I don my wet suit and dive with Abby for lobsters. In the water I forget my stomach and take a deep breath, diving down deep among the rocks, peering into holes. A black-and-orange tentacle shows. Up again to the surface, cocking the sling I carry, now back down under, deeper now, facing the entrance of the hole, holding myself in position with one hand as the sea is swaying me. I am running out of air; I lose a moment watching a purple sea fan wave. I move closer, the hole comes into focus, I point my sling, which will pierce him, and let fly. Got him! No. He pulls free and swims out a back entrance to his hole and is gone. I burst up to the surface for air, then down again, diving over and over until exhausted. Finally, I give up the hunt and take a long, slow swim, watching the seabed swirl beneath me as I float for shore. When I get out of the water, I too am sick with turista and collapse in my bag with chills and nausea in the high winds and heat of the afternoon sun, dreaming of whales singing and my grandmother's house.

Late that afternoon we travel a short distance to our next campsite, where Abby and Lucie will leave us. None of us are well but we decide to go on. There are not many options. This area is very remote. I've been asked to be the leader of our small-group expedition. I am pleased

Gull Rock

to have a role clear cut. Assistant-instructor/student/group-organizer proves to be a motley mix of roles. It is a relief to be clearly just one kind of person for the next three days.

We review our emergency procedures. How will we carry out an evacuation these next few days if we need to? This is where leadership is crucial. An emergency: you must be decisive, efficient, and accurate in your assessment of need, safety, and the assignment of tasks. Here one person must clearly be in charge with everyone cooperating. With most of us debilitated by the turista, we are weak to start with, myself included. There will be no one with us who can easily identify the coves that are safe to pull into from our hundred-year-old map. Abby redraws another point where the map is inaccurate and the tension grows. Once again over the next twenty-five miles we will have to cross a stretch with no pull-in in case of high winds. We carry no food, agreeing to eat only what we can catch ourselves, though Abby gives me a small emergency supply in case of an accident.

If we have an accident, the Mexican fishermen in their motorboats are our first source of help. If we can signal one. I saw one this morning, a lone fisherman standing in his blue boat. Or we can send a runner for miles across the desert. With only five of us in the group, we are taking our chances and must rely totally on one another. There is no slack. The three people who drowned last spring were on a final expedition, too, though with another school, not NOLS. The weight of everyone's life, including my own, feels massive. Yet I feel ready. It's time. I can do this.

Abby and Lucie set out to leave just before sunset, after one last demonstration of boat repair. Suddenly the parting is upon us and we are freed from the burden of our previous relationships as students and instructors. The tensions ease; they are friends; we are our own group with our own leader. A warmth surges up as we part with big hugs all around. They let go; we are on our own.

Happy to be by ourselves, we relish the freedom of making our own decisions. We build a fire and like the Indians give each other names taken from the environment that remind us of each person. Names like Endless Summer, Steady Wind.

At twilight we gather to examine the shells we've collected: princely cones, herites, chocolates, cowries, periwinkles, scallops, chitons, conchs, coffee beans, *almeja de sangre*, the blood clam; these are the names.

San Basilio Bay

MARCH 19

San Basilio. Now the larger adventure begins. This is the first day we travel on our own.

Here I've come up the hillside to watch the clouds. The wind is strong, steady from the northeast, the horizon choppy with whitecaps. It's six-thirty in the morning. Clouds slowly drift from the southwest and billow up. A single dove lights on the cactus nearby. Gulls, osprey, grebes, oystercatchers, kites, red-tailed hawks, and turkey vultures fly by. Each morning we are greeted by a single sweet descending note. Though I can never see the bird that sings this song, I know that it must be a canyon wren. I have heard that note many times deep in the canyons of the Rio Grande and the Colorado. The desert country: I am at home when I hear the canyon wren.

Now when we depart the moon is half full, setting overland behind the coastal mountains while the sun rises over the sea. Here, on the Sea of Cortez, when the moon is full, it rises up red, elliptical, almost bursting, unwilling to part from the sea.

Behind us Pulpito floats loose from the land in the distance: it becomes an island with Isla Tortuga suspended beyond, inches above the water's surface. Sight contradicts reason at sea.

MARCH 20

Punta Manglese

On our way to Punta Manglese we see a large whale. First she blows in the distance, then sounds and reappears a few hundred feet away. We stop paddling and sit quietly in our boats. Red and brown cliffs rise steep at our backs, the sea is calm, and we are caught up in the close presence of so large a creature. We can't tell what kind of whale it is, possibly an orca or a finback. All is quiet. The whale has sounded. Then she blows again and stays close by. A slick black surface shows just above the water, then the spray from the blowhole, then down again. In the moving water, we cannot tell from the whale motion whether there is one whale or a mother and a calf. Within fifteen minutes, the whale is gone. We paddle on though reluctant to leave the spot. Here we are the curiosities, suspended on the sea, nothing between us, no separation, part of the natural world for a time. Here, we are clearly participants in the natural world.

Weakened by turista, we fail to catch the lobster that we see all around us. This afternoon we grow hungry. Sally persuades us to look for edible plants. Robin and I take off into the desert heading for the cholla cactus. Lunch consists of the cholla fruit: hard, cucumbery, sour and green. Marilyn saves the day by catching a chino mero fish in the late afternoon. Dinner is three bites of chino mero in broth, a hatful of berries, and a bitter cup of creosote tea, which we promptly spit out. Creosote tea was used by the Indians to heal wounds and cure illnesses. I'd prefer it on a wound.

Though we don't talk about it, the reality is that each of us knows an unspoken agreement to provide the group with food. Whether we are well or not, whether we are successful or not, we all attempt to gather food.

There is something crazy and wonderful about this band of five women depending on one another for food and life itself. While diving, if one of us is bitten by one of the moray eels that inhabit the rocks where

we search for lobster, our partner will have to unsheath her knife and cut off the eel's head. Moray eels' jaws are fiercely muscled and unyielding. Diving in pairs, each of us counts on the other to save her from drowning. If we are hungry, it is one of our own who feeds us, having caught, killed, and cooked the food, having gathered the wood and built the fire. We have gone back to the basics of being alive.

On the next day, the weakness from turista is compounded with growing hunger. Diving takes a great deal of energy. With all of us in varying degrees of recovery, we have been able to catch only the smallest amounts of food. Still the feeling of self-sufficiency is growing. I know how to catch my own food and feed myself and those I'm responsible for. Whether I do it successfully every time doesn't matter. I have gained a certain kind of essential knowledge. The rest is a matter of practice.

We build a fire in the shelter of some rocks. Sally sits across from me, smiling so wide that her blue eyes seem like lakes on the brown ground of her face. Her shadow grows in the firelight. We talk about women who have been models for us. Models, heroes, heroines, who have they been so far? For Sally, Amelia Earhart; for her mother, Eleanor Roosevelt. For Sheila, Annie Oakley; for Marilyn, Ayn Rand. For me, it changes; now it's Helen Caldicott, or Laura Bonaparte of Amnesty International, or the medieval Christian mystic Julian of Norwich, who spoke of God as our mother. Our talk goes on late. We say goodnight, drawing our sleeping bags up by the fire.

I lie by the fire in Baja realizing that even here there is no escape from the dilemmas we have created with chemical and nuclear wastes in the environment. Like a mind loosed from its body, technology forgets that the destruction it can produce may be its own. It floats at sea like Pulpito in the distance, but in truth it is a part of the shore.

As I write now I wonder, Is this getting off the subject of Baja? What is the subject of Baja? The journey and the vision, bringing it back home. It's easy to leave and have an adventure, to have a glimpse of another way of life; we all do when we go away. But for me the goal is to bring this image home, to keep it alive, let it run, spill over, and shape everyday life. These journeys are passages, ritual observances of a deeper time and place.

San Bruno

MARCH 21

This morning we paddle to San Bruno, our takeout point, and arrive at eight-forty-five in the morning. The weather is excellent. The cliffs we pass are striking in their contrasts of red, black, white, buff, ochre, and brown. We pull in to the southern end of the beach to face an unrelenting wind from the west. It's good to be off the water. At the northwest point of this beach is a Mexican fishing camp, with a red-and-white-striped tent tucked into the rocks, flanked by the Jesuit date palms. As always, the fishermen are friendly, but they are busy and have a full day's work ahead of them, so they nod politely, wish us good day and go on with their work.

This is the third and last day of the small group expedition. At ten-thirty in the morning having no one to dive with, I decide to go fishing. Marilyn fishes too. Sally and Robin strike out into the chaparral to find edible plants, Sheila reads. We spend a quiet day and agree not to be disheartened if again we have little or nothing to eat.

We have had good fortune. Each of us has depended on the others for her own safety. If one of us hadn't assessed her own condition accurately, and had weakened while at sea, we could all have been endangered. The lessons here are many. I lose my fishing lure on the rocks while casting and can't retrieve it. Now I have to give it up altogether and I'm relieved of the pressure to provide. I need time to digest so much learning.

Our camp at San Bruno is by a small lagoon which brings life to the desert around it. A wild burro walks through to his watering hole, which is fringed with bright green pickleweed. Behind us looms the mountain range called the Sierra de la Giganta. Returning to camp, I plunge into plant identification again, wanting to absorb as much lore as I can while here, reluctant to leave my desert home. Marilyn returns with a single fish.

MARCH 22

Early, the owl hoots deep in the desert and the sky is tinged with pink. I wake with dreams of elaborate stories printed on tiny bird feathers; feathered stories to be read only with a magnifying glass. As the sun rises a big storm builds around the Sierra de la Giganta. The dark storm clouds are underlit with the red of the morning sun. The sun comes up fast now, dazzling, warming this desert life, and with it come the bird songs. For a moment the world takes on a glow of pinks and purples, the greens turn electric. This early light, already changing, passes from pink to orange to bright yellow. The wind comes up and riffles the lagoon. Abby and Lucie arrive in the blue pickup. The expedition is finished.

> *Our bones are lightning*
> *in the night of flesh.*
> *O world, all is night,*
> *life is the lightning.*
>
> —JOSEPH WOOD KRUTCH,
> *Baja, The Geography of Hope*

III   How We Got There

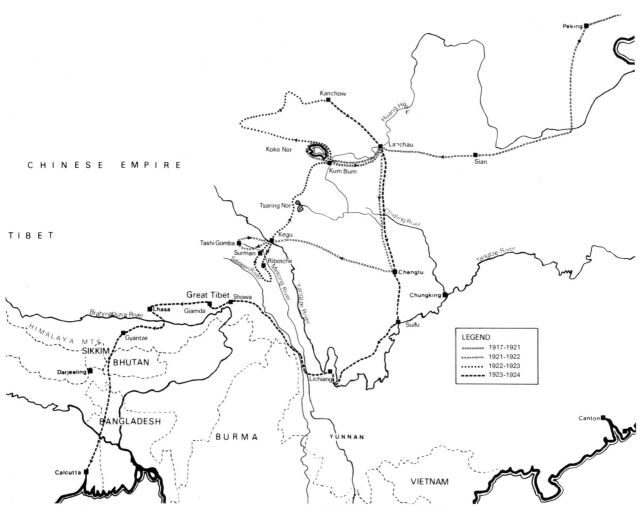

Map of Alexandra David-Néel's routes, 1917–1924

III

How We Got There
women adventurers of the past

lexandra David-Néel, the nineteenth-century explorer, has long intrigued me. Born in France in 1868, David-Néel was a prodigious traveler, writer, and scholar of Tibetan Buddhism. She became famous in her day because of her journey to Lhasa, the forbidden capital of Tibet and home of the Dalai Lama. Tibet had been closed by the Chinese but Alexandra gained entry by traveling from China through Mongolia and across the Gobi Desert into Tibet, disguised as a Tibetan beggar. She wrote over twenty books and numerous articles recounting her travels and adventures and the results of her long study and practice of Tibetan Buddhism. *Magic and Mystery in Tibet, Initiations and Initiates in Tibet, My Journey to Lhasa*— these and others of her books are available again today.

I skim *Magic and Mystery*, check over maps of her route, comparing them with the itinerary we plan for a Buddhist studies trek into Nepal. Will my path cross David-Néel's? It is impossible to tell. Many of her routes as she journeyed through India, China, Nepal, Sikkim, and Tibet over the years remain unknown. My interest grows when I discover that the Buddhist scholar Lama Anagarika Govinda and his wife, the painter Li Gotima, knew Alexandra briefly in India. Through the Govindas I am able to learn something about her more directly.

Alexandra David-Néel led an unconventional, long, and productive life, working vigorously until her death at 101 on September 8, 1969. Luree Miller's valuable book *On Top of the World: Five Women Explorers in Tibet* provides an account of David-Néel and four other nineteenth-century women explorers.* Of David-Néel she says:

> Her life had begun obscurely, and was nearly lost in the destructive morass of despair. Then belatedly, she burst forth in a full flowering beyond any early expectations. At the crisis point of her life, in her mid-thirties, Alexandra confronted the problem of fulfilling her potential. With unusual self-knowledge she chose the right path for the realization of her

---

* Except as noted, quoted material in this account of A. David-Néel is excerpted from Luree Miller's *On Top of the World.*

Alexandra David-Néel

rare talents: a path without guideposts, fraught with obstacles
and adventures few women have ever encountered.

"Despair," "crisis," "flowering," "path without guideposts": I want
to know more. Wondering what moved her to write her book, I write
to Luree Miller. She replies:

> I became interested in such a book while I was living in
> Pakistan and India (1957–64). On musty back shelves of second-
> hand bookstores, I found books of letters or memoirs of
> Victorian women who loved the sub-continent (as memsahibs
> were alleged not to have) and who had traveled alone or with
> a small expedition. It seemed to me that a record should be
> made of these attractive and enterprising women so that
> women adventurers could begin to establish their own
> tradition. Also, I wanted to counter the misconception of
> Western women in Asia as the embodiment of all the worst
> elements of colonialism. Some were, of course, but not all sat
> home scolding their native servants. And I felt a kinship with
> those who did not—especially when I trekked in Nepal.

Alexandra David-Néel was born a Catholic and raised in convent
schools. She ran away several times as a young girl, even considering
becoming a Carmelite nun, but left the Church when she became
interested in comparative religion.

In Paris, Alexandra would retreat from the world and pore over books on the East at the Musée Guimet. She claimed that her vocation was born there. While she was in her early twenties, a small inheritance from her godmother allowed her to travel to India and Ceylon (Sri Lanka).

Having no income, she had to return to France to earn her living. This necessity was complicated by the fact that women had few legal rights at that time. She supported herself by becoming a successful opera singer during the 1890s, traveling with a variety of opera companies. But in 1903 she left the theater life for good and took up journalism. She wrote in both French and English, usually about Buddhism and the East. In Tunis she met her future husband, Phillipe-François Néel, a distant cousin. She and Phillipe married but within five days she sailed for Europe and they went their separate ways.

From examining David-Néel's diary Miller concludes that marriage must have seemed like a prison to a woman who had lived so independently, supporting herself until the age of thirty-six. When Alexandra left for Paris, Phillipe left for southern France. To her diary she admitted that all was over and that she had lost her freedom. Though she and Phillipe would visit periodically from then on, they were never to really live together.

After a traumatic, near-suicidal period following her father's death, Alexandra went to London, Phillipe to North Africa. She would have no children, she informed her husband, though she remained his wife. He continued to help support her until the end of his life forty years later. They corresponded, he handled her business transactions, had her articles typed and sent to the designated journals. Her will was formidable, enabling her to survive her identity crisis. Though never divorced, she shed the bonds of marriage and family and created her own way of life.

For the next six years after their marriage, Alexandra continued to write, study, and travel in Europe, making an occasional visit to Phillipe in Tunisia. She studied Sanskrit at the Sorbonne, lectured at the Theosophical Societies in London and Paris, but finally left again for India at the age of forty-two. She explained to Phillipe in a letter upon her departure in 1911: "I wish to live philosophy on the spot and undergo physical and spiritual training, not just read about them."

Once back in India, she decided that an interview with the Dalai Lama, the spiritual leader of Tibetan Buddhists, would be of interest to her readers in Europe. At that time he was living in exile from Tibet. She became the first Western woman ever to be granted an audience with him.

The Dalai Lama had been forced out of Tibet by a Chinese invasion in 1910 and was living in Darjeeling. He was greatly impressed with this Western woman who knew so much about Buddhism and

A woman's education must therefore be planned in relation to man. To be pleasing in his sight, to win his respect and love, to train him in childhood, to tend him in manhood, to counsel and console, to make his life pleasant and happy, these are the duties of woman for all time, and this is what she should be taught while she is young.
—EVA FIGES, *Patriarchal Attitudes*

We don't want our wives and daughters to be mathematicians, philosophers, or scientists. We don't love and honor them for what they know of such things, but rather for what they don't know.
—ANONYMOUS U.S. CONGRESSMAN, 1870s, in Nancy Wilson Ross, *Westward the Women*

Women beware. You are on the brink of destruction: You have hitherto been engaged in crushing your waists; now you are attempting to cultivate your mind; you have been merely dancing all night in the foul air of the ballroom; now you are beginning to spend your mornings in study. You have been incessantly stimulating your emotions with concerts and operas, with French plays, and French novels; now you are exerting your understanding to learn Greek, and solve propositions in Euclid. Beware!!! Science pronounces that the woman who studies is lost.
—R. R. COLEMAN, M.D., 1880s, in Ehrenreich and English, *For Her Own Good*

encouraged her to learn the Tibetan language to further her studies. Alexandra hardly needed the encouragement.

From Darjeeling Alexandra traveled to Sikkim, where she befriended the crown prince, who was also a lama. The crown prince, who had studied at Oxford, agreed to assist her in her studies of Tibetan. How Alexandra could enter a country and meet with royalty Miller does not tell us. One assumes that her presence was so unusual that, particularly in a country as tiny as Sikkim, she would be sought out by everyone. Furthermore, she stayed on in Sikkim as a guest of the prince, visiting villages and monasteries and lecturing to monks as she traveled through the countryside. She wrote to Phillipe of the Sikkimese attitude toward a woman who was pursuing a course of study. Here she was treated with great respect and taken seriously. In France, at the Sorbonne, she recalled, police protection was sometimes required for women students, so greatly were they reviled. Alexandra admitted to Phillipe the difficulty of supporting herself and some of her journey's hardships that she fails to communicate to her readers. Miller, with access to Alexandra and Phillipe's correspondence, gives the reader a flavor of Alexandra's travels that isn't evident in her own books.

Like the rest of us, David-Néel had her difficulties, went through periods of great struggle and despair. She is exciting for the very fact that she was able to live through and turn around her interior turmoil.

She parted company with the prince and his court, though she continued to travel through the Himalayan foothills. It was at this time that she took on Yongden, then a boy of fifteen. He was a young Tibetan who started out as her personal attendant but became her companion until his death forty years later. She was twenty-nine years his senior and considered him her son. When she returned to France years later, Yongden was in tow, and was legally adopted by Phillipe, who objected to the whole idea, however. As usual, Alexandra's will prevailed.

When the war broke out in Europe in 1914, Alexandra gave up the idea of going home. Though it was illegal, she slipped across the border into Tibet from Sikkim. There she discovered a small band of nuns at the monastery of Chorten Nyima. In *Magic and Mystery in Tibet*, she writes of the differences between women, East and West:

> . . . what astonished me was the tranquil courage of the womenfolk. Very few Western women would dare to live in the desert, in groups of four or five or sometimes quite alone. Few would dare under such conditions to undertake journeys that last for months or even years, through solitary mountain regions infested by wild beasts and brigands.

Alexandra went on to discover that communities of fewer than a dozen nuns each were scattered throughout the mountains of Tibet, some of them blocked in by snow six months of the year.

Jungul Himal, the Himalayas

> Other women live as hermits in caves and many women
> pilgrims travel alone, across the immense territory of Tibet
> carrying their scanty luggage on their backs. . . . This shows
> the singular character of Tibetan women.

Alexandra heard of a famous hermit lama from some of the nuns
she had met in the mountains. She set out to find him and inquired
whether she could become his student. He gave her a small cave of
her own not far down the mountainside from his and was persuaded
within a week or so to accept her as his student. Yongden and their
servants were in a hut nearby. She had to promise not to leave her
retreat until released by the lama. According to my conversation with
Lama Govinda, who knew this *gomchen*, or teacher, she stayed three
years.

The lama told Govinda years later that she was indeed quite
remarkable and had been one of his most excellent students. Both
Govinda and the *gomchen* expressed amazement over this European
woman's choosing to live in a cave for three years. But apparently
Alexandra loved it and learned Tibetan with a native accent as well
as a great deal of Tibetan Buddhism. The strangeness of the experience
"aroused my enthusiasm," Alexandra wrote characteristically. She
described her life as a hermit as intensely "voluptuous" and "peculiar."
The richness of the memories from this time, her long walks through
the forests stayed deep within her for the rest of her life.

Then it was springtime in the cloudy Himalaya. Nine hundred feet below my cave rhododendrons blossomed. I climbed barren mountain-tops. Long tramps led me to desolate valleys studded with translucent lakes. . . . Solitude, solitude! . . . Mind and sense develop their sensibility in this contemplative life made up of continual observations and reflections. Does one become a visionary or, rather, is it not that one has been blind until then?
—ALEXANDRA DAVID-NÉEL

How great was the mental transformation necessary to enable me to become, a few years later, a joyful tramp in the wilds of Tibet.
—ALEXANDRA DAVID-NÉEL

Released by the lama, she left the mountain hermitage, and not long after her return to Sikkim she was ordered to leave for having illegally slipped across the border. This action infuriated Alexandra and roused her inborn rebelliousness. "What decided me to go to Lhasa was above all the absurd prohibition which closes Tibet." Ousted from Sikkim, apparently on her way back to India, she now would have to enter Tibet through China, which was racked by civil wars. This did not seem to deter Alexandra and Yongden, though it made travel even more difficult than usual.

Her routes become impossible to trace. Much of the country that she crossed on her journey to Lhasa was not mapped. She went through Mongolia, across the Gobi Desert. The dangers of being robbed or shot or dying of exposure were all quite real, and she and Yongden confronted all of the possibilities on their way.

She had taken up the challenge of reaching the forbidden capital and was "now ready to show what a woman could do." At age fifty-five, the former opera star cast herself as a Tibetan beggar woman on a pilgrimage to Lhasa with her priestly son. She darkened her hair with ink, and her face with cocoa and charcoal; she added yak hair braids, looped earrings, and a Tibetan robe.

Alexandra David-Néel told Phillipe many times that she was "a solitaire." She was to write him later before her return to Europe, "I am a savage. . . . I love only my tent, my horses and the desert." Her wildness served her well on her journey.

Traveling for months, she finally stole across the Chinese-Tibetan border, climbing mountains, some of which are unnamed to this day, going over numerous passes, some as high as twenty thousand feet. The spectacular terrain was often treacherous.

Her fluency in the native language kept her from being discovered. She followed behind her "son" Yongden the monk, and no one paid attention to her. Life as a beggar and peasant woman could hardly have been more in contrast to her former days as a "lady lama" lecturing at monasteries. And yet she seemed to thrive upon it all and viewed it as a wonderful game. "To the one who knows how to look and feel, every moment of this free wandering life is an enchantment."

Finally she and Yongden reached Lhasa at the time of the New Year's festival, which helped conceal her entrance to the city. She joined the crowds, sat on the walls watching the festivities, bargained with vendors, bought books, and enjoyed herself thoroughly. But the magnificent Potala, the fortress palace of the exiled Dalai Lama, was her goal. Pilgrims were allowed in during the festival, so she and Yongden entered after engaging some villagers to go with him while she followed behind, the old beggar woman.

She was not disappointed. The Potala was magnificent, filled, room after room, with enormous gold, silver, and copper images of the Buddha. The shrines were draped in silk banners of the mystical colors of white, green, red, blue, and yellow.

Lama Govinda recalled the story of his friend a Tibetan general, who was chief of the Dalai Lama's guards. Though her disguise was excellent, the general noticed Alexandra's European blue eyes during a procession. She knew she had been discovered and left Lhasa shortly thereafter. According to Miller, she was able to remain there two months before her return to India, whereupon she immediately let the Chinese government know that it had been unable to restrict her travel after all.

In her letters to Phillipe and only there, Miller says, Alexandra admitted to the madness of her journey. Upon reaching Lhasa her health was failing. She was light-headed with fever, and more often than she wanted to remember she had had no idea where she was. She had learned well that experience provides the only reliable guide and, as her teacher assured her, truth is a matter that one can only discover for oneself. Her convictions, her rebellious streak, and her wildness had carried her through the trials of the journey. Once back in India she recovered and was flushed with success.

Alexandra David-Néel and Yongden

At long last, after fourteen years, Alexandra began to prepare to return home. She instructed Phillipe to contact the press and make her accomplishments known. Ever her faithful friend, he did so and readied himself as best he could for her return. They both had misgivings about her ability to live in the Western world again.

Upon her return, she was rightly accorded the status of an authority on Tibetan Buddhism. She continued to write prolifically, both books and articles, and lectured throughout Europe. For the next ten years Phillipe would visit her periodically, and they continued to be close.

In 1938 when she was nearly seventy, Alexandra returned to China. Money was still a struggle, no matter how many articles she wrote about news in China. Three years later, while she was still in the East, Phillipe died. She was disconsolate, saying that she "had lost the best of husbands . . . and her only friend."

In 1944, she and Yongden returned to France. Her home there was called Samten Dzong, Fortress of Meditation. She continued her life vigorously. In 1955, Yongden died, yet David-Néel carried on, writing and receiving the scholars and admirers who visited until her death, in 1969, at 101.

I stop reading and wander down to our house from my cabin for a cup of coffee. Waiting for the water to boil, I ponder the change in

"Om Mani Padme Om," Tibetan prayer-rock painting

spirits that has come over me since beginning to read about Alexandra and other nineteenth-century women. Their life stories display the triumph of implacable spirit, the danger and the merit of following one's own path, and the realities of living out a dream. All encountered obstacles and hardships on their paths, whether they started on their journeys well financed or penniless. All confronted dangers and hardships that no background, money, or status could soften. Their determination and conviction were compelling; their willingness to accept and confront difficulty rather than retreat from it reminds me that I can do that in my own life.

Another woman I have heard of ever since coming to California is Isabella Bird Bishop. An Englishwoman, she spent time traveling alone by horseback in and out of California's and Colorado's mining and pioneer towns in the late 1800s. Her book *A Lady's Life in the Rocky Mountains* is one of nine travel books she published, each a best seller. Almost all of her books have been republished and are currently available. She is also included in Luree Miller's *On Top of the World.**

I am amused no end to read that when Isabella Bird Bishop was at home in Edinburgh, attempting to settle into the proper life of a lady, her health would fail. Frail health was virtually synonymous with the

* Quoted material in this account of I. B. Bishop is excerpted from *On Top of the World.*

status of a "lady" in the nineteenth century. Of course, poorer women had much better health; they needed it.

Isabella had poor health from childhood and was operated on at eighteen to remove a tumor from her spine. Her condition failed to improve and as a last resort the doctors prescribed travel. Once she was abroad her health rapidly became better. Her letters home proved to be of such lively interest that they were kept by her family and she published them upon her return. So began her writing career. But as soon as she was home in Edinburgh her health began to give out again, so travel again was prescribed.

This time she stayed away longer, almost a year, traveling and writing about the religious revival in America. During this time, her health was good, she produced another successful book, then returned to Edinburgh where she stayed with her sister, Hennie. But gradually over the years she began to develop insomnia and became deeply depressed, in addition to having more difficulty with her spine. Medical care was of no avail. Soon her regular cruise to New York didn't help, and she was ordered to take a lengthy trip. At thirty-seven, Bishop was quite ill and depressed.

She set sail for the Sandwich Islands. During the voyage there was a storm that threatened to break up the ship. Drowning was suddenly a possibility, and this seems to have been the event that turned her life around. Isabella explained to her sister, Hennie, in a letter home that she had been won over by the spirit of the sea. "To me it is like living in a new world, so free, so fresh, so vital, so careless, so unfettered, so full of interest that one grudges being asleep." She was transformed from a sickly spinster into an indefatigable world traveler. But Isabella was no hedonist, Miller points out. She was forever "making up" for not staying at home and leading a conventional life. She began to travel around the world. But when at home she would lecture to the YMCA and to church groups; make soup to take to the sick; and give to charitable causes.

While on one of her travels, she visited Hawaii and discovered women there riding horses astride like men, rather than side saddle, which was considered proper for a lady. She followed suit, and not long afterward came to San Francisco, rented a horse, and for four months traveled alone through California and Colorado mining and cattle camps, helping with cleaning and cooking, learning to drive a wagon and to round up cattle. Then she returned to Edinburgh, to her sister's cottage, wrote two more books, and then was off again, this time to Japan and Malaya.

At fifty, she married Dr. John Bishop, ten years her junior. Her spinal problems continued to plague her; her husband became ill himself and died shortly before their fifth anniversary. Her beloved sister, Hennie, had died just before Isabella's marriage; now she was alone in the world.

Live as domestic a life as possible. Have your child with you all the time.

Lie down an hour after each meal. Have but two hours intellectual life a day. And never touch pen, brush or pencil as long as you live.
—DR. S. WEIR MITCHELL, 1880s, a "female specialist" to Charlotte Perkins Gilman

Certain women seek to rival men in manly sports . . . and the strong-minded ape them in all things, even in dress. In doing so they may command a sort of admiration such as all monstrous productions inspire, especially when they tend toward a higher type than their own.
—President of the American Medical Association, 1871, in Ehrenreich and English, *For Her Own Good*

LONG'S PEAK, COLORADO

From it comes all storms of snow and wind, and the forked lightnings play round its head like glory. It is one of the noblest of mountains, but in one's imagination it grows to be much more than a mountain. It becomes invested with a personality. In its caverns and abysses one comes to fancy that it generates and chains the strong winds, to let them loose in its fury. The thunder becomes its voice, and the lightnings do it homage.

—ISABELLA BIRD BISHOP, from her journal

At fifty-five, she took up nursing and went overseas to found missionary hospitals in Kashmir, Pakistan, and China, in memory of her sister and husband. Eventually she too would travel extensively in Tibet.

She was a keen observer and wrote constantly throughout her travels. Miller notes that during the travels to the East Bishop was horrified by the corruption of Buddhism and the oppression of women in the Islamic countries. She did not fail to record her feelings.

Later, when she traveled in Persia, her abhorrence of the Muslim practices of seclusion of women and polygamy was deepened by her experience.

> These faiths degrade women [she asserted]. The intellect is dwarfed, while also all the worst passions of human nature are stimulated and developed to a fearful degree; jealousy, envy, murder, hatred, intrigue running to such an extent that, in some countries, I have hardly ever been in a woman's house, or near a woman's tent, without being asked for drugs with which to disfigure the favorite wife, to take away her life, or to take away the life of the favorite wife's infant son.

Her books and world travels brought her a great deal of success. At the age of sixty-one, she was elected a fellow of the Royal Geographical Society. Though her health was still considered poor, she continued to travel, taking off again at the age of sixty-three for Japan, China, and Korea for a three-year stay.

She traveled on horseback, sometimes through blizzards over mountain passes. Nothing could stop her.

Bishop's fearlessness and endurance were formidable. She returned to England again for a round of lectures, writing, and visiting friends, only to turn around again at the age of seventy in 1901 and make one final and spectacular gesture, a thousand-mile ride through Morocco. She rode from Tangier to Marrakesh to wish the Sultan of Morocco "long life and happiness." The Sultan replied that he wished for her energy when he reached her age. Her extravagant gesture touches me as I see her in the distance on horseback, age seventy, vigorous spirit, still so full of life, riding among the Berbers. She died in 1904 at the age of seventy-three.

Miller cites an article that appeared after Isabella's death that strikes the contrast one needs to see here. While at home in Edinburgh she was described as fragile and dependent; abroad she was indifferent to danger and fatigue. Here are the paradoxes in Isabella's character. And her story makes me wonder how many Isabellas exist today.

Sent West on assignment for a magazine story in the early 1940s, Nancy Wilson Ross came across stories of women during the frontier

days that she collected and put into her book *Westward the Women.**
Also known for her novels and texts on Buddhism, Nancy recalled her
excitement in discovering these stories when we met at the Zen Center
not long ago. The women she writes of range from missionary wives
left to fend for themselves much of the time in the isolated countryside,
to "Ada Mercer's girls," who sailed around Cape Horn to help end
the shortage of women on the frontier, to a brave band of nuns who
settled in the Northwest, to the famous Indian woman Sacajawea. Two
of these frontier women, Abigail Scott Duniway and Bethenia Owen,
caught my eye. Later the elements of my attraction to them became
more obvious to me. Like me, both were mothers who had to assume
financial responsibility for their families, both chose to do so
unconventionally, and both had the experience in childhood of
disappointing their families by not being born male. The wilderness
they entered was social: the rough and tumble town and countryside
of pioneer days.

I was pleased to discover their stories, and I imagine that a great
many women have had similar childhood experiences. Both Abigail Scott
Duniway and Bethenia Owen were born into families that had long
awaited sons. In my own case, I was simply the first born, with younger
brothers to come five years later, and long suspected that my parents
had wanted me to be a boy. As an adolescent, I found my mother's
diary. The entry on my birthday noted her initial disappointment that
she had not borne a son. The next sentence added that the
disappointment was momentary. But as an adolescent I imagined that
I had found "proof" of the charge I was wont to level at them.

Did my parents want me to be a boy or did I want to be one because
I found the male realm to be more interesting and exciting as I grew
up? In our society, where men have more access to power, more mobility
and control, it is not surprising that many girls experience this vague
sense of diminution on their way to becoming women.

Despite the enormous efforts of many people, achievements of
women's suffrage and other "advances," I have to wonder about what
can really be called progress. The ongoing fight over the passsage of
the Equal Rights Amendment has dragged out interminably because
the real issues are nonrational and can't be legislated. It is clear that
we must have the laws and must pass the Equal Rights Amendment,
but as soon as you scratch the surface it feels as if we're still in the
nineteenth century. Just the other evening a newscaster was saying that
scientists are working on being able to choose the sex of a child before

---

* For the following accounts of Abigail Scott Duniway, Bethenia Owen, and Mary
Richardson, I have relied on Nancy Ross's stories.

pregnancy. The news is that parents still prefer boys, and the forecast is for fewer females.

Abigail Scott Duniway moved to Oregon with her family in the 1850s; she was destined to become "one of the most reviled and eventually one of the most respected" women of the West.

Early in her life, she was stung by her mother's disappointment in producing a daughter when a son was lacking in the family. According to Ross, her mother's disappointment was a painful blow and started her questioning woman's lot. Later Abigail herself had five sons and one daughter, to whom she was particularly close.

Circumstance forced Abigail into the role of sole supporter of herself, an invalid husband, and six children. What for many people would have been intolerable calamities, including the loss of a family farm, became Abigail's motivations. She moved her family to town, taught school, saved $30 and went into business for herself.

In her characteristically direct manner, Abigail took her money and went to Portland to seek the advice of Jacob Meier, the richest merchant in town, on how to open up her own millinery and notions shop in Albany. Millinery was one of the few occupations available to nineteenth-century women that paid a living wage. Meier was so impressed with Abigail that upon parting he insisted she take $1200 worth of goods on credit. Ross tells us that within three weeks Abigail returned to Meier, paid off her initial debt, and left with $3000 more worth of goods for her shop. She had launched a successful business.

Business thrust her directly into the mainstream of town life. As a milliner, she was constantly in the company and confidence of women and was infuriated by what she saw: women, with no allowances or financial independence, stealing change from their husbands' pants at night to buy themselves or their daughters hats. Their situation was not altogether unlike the situation Isabella Bird Bishop found Islamic women in. Husbands would also steal their wives' "butter money," the single pittance women could glean in the countryside. Women had no rights, no recourse. After hearing their stories over and over again, Abigail recalled later that her husband had convinced her that nothing could change the situation of women until they had the right to vote and were afforded equal rights before the law. So, at the age of thirty-six, Abigail chose woman suffrage as her life's work. It seems that these nineteenth-century women had extraordinarily forward-thinking or tolerant husbands.

In 1871 Duniway sold her shop and moved her family to Portland. She set her sons up to learn printing and founded a newspaper for women, *The New Northwest*. Her accomplishment thrust her into the company of leading suffragettes Susan B. Anthony and Elizabeth Cady Stanton. Her paper was successful, read by friend and foe alike. Soon she took to speaking publicly on women's rights, and endured for many years the hardships that entailed. At that time, public speaking by women was almost completely unacceptable. Her traveling companions were mostly men and "sporting women," and that company gave her an unsavory reputation that she was able to live with only by virtue of her sense of humor. Ross describes well the difficulties she encountered, such as how she would often have to sleep in a corner with the children in a strange house, or sit up all night since there was no place for her to go after dark.

"The wonder was," said Abigail as an old woman, "that anyone should have been endowed with sufficient courage to endure and persevere in her demand for women's enfranchisement."

In 1912, Abigail signed the Equal Suffrage Proclamation for the State of Oregon, a document she had written herself. This was "an event as significant in the long unrecorded history of women as the writing of the Constitution was to humanity in general," Ross states.

In her later years, Abigail Scott Duniway cautioned young women to remember the work that had been done to gain their freedom:

> The young women of today, free to study, to speak, to write, to choose their occupation, should remember that every inch of this freedom was bought for them at a great price. It is for them to show their gratitude by helping onward the reforms of their own time by spreading the light of freedom and of truth still wider.

Leading the quiet life of a minister's wife, Mary Richardson lived far from the hubbub of town, in the wilderness of the Northwest Territory. Working from Richardson's journal, Ross gives us a sketch of what a woman's life was like in pioneer days. Her work day averaged sixteen hours and could include ironing; carpentry; roof and chimney repair; milking; making soap, butter, and all the family garments, including shoes. As a missionary's wife, Mary Richardson also attempted to teach the Indians about Christianity and about the world at large. She gave geography lessons and used painted eggshells to represent the globe.

And yet, in the midst of family life with eight children, Mary made time to learn geology, mineralogy, and botany. A wandering botanist would help her learn from her dried plant collection. An itinerant painter taught her about birds. She took up taxidermy despite her husband's protests, and her journal records stuffing cranes, partridges, salmon, and ducks. But, at the end of her portrait of Mary Richardson, Ross asks a hard question, "What happens when you cannot find other minds with which to shape your questions and your findings?" This was a problem for women then and still is for many today. What happened to Mary Richardson was that her mind failed. In the end

> *None of them of course could read the future, or could have known in that day that women truly are the most conservative of creatures, hating with a passion those three concomitants of the western frontier—poverty, physical hardship, and danger.*
>
> —DEE BROWN,
> *Gentle Tamers*, 1968

"she would spend hours in the old sidesaddle, placed on a chair, rocking with her traveling cape around her."

Bethenia Owen, another of the frontier women Ross writes about, lived a life which set some landmarks on the trail to womanhood. Although this nineteenth-century milliner turned doctor lived a hundred years before me, I found much to identify with in her story.

A bride at fourteen, Bethenia left her husband after a little over three years of marriage when he whipped their sick infant for crying too much. By the time she was eighteen she was back in her father's house, divorced, broken in health and spirit, with a two-year-old child. Her feeling that she would "never be happy or strong again" is familiar to me. At twenty-one, I divorced my first husband and returned to my father's house, seven months pregnant with my daughter, holding my one-year-old son in my arms. I too felt broken, and spent ten days in a Boston hospital on the verge of miscarriage.

Bethenia's solution to her despair was to go to school immediately, even though that meant attending with younger brothers and sisters. She taught school as well, in addition to supporting herself and her child by whatever manner of work came along, whether it was washing clothes or picking berries. During these years, Ross tells us, Bethenia set up a routine which she kept to for the rest of her life, a discipline which I'm sure had a great deal to do with her later happiness and success. She would rise early and take a cold bath and would exercise vigorously every day.

When she finished school, she too entered millinery. In between making hats she began to study *Gray's Anatomy*. At thirty-two, she announced to family and friends that she was headed East to study medicine. They discouraged her and told her she was disgracing them, but she refused to give in. She left, with her son, returning later as a doctor. Being one of the few women doctors in the Northwest brought its own trials and hardships. But she was on her own and eventually established herself, earning respect in the community. Her perseverance and drive encourage me.

Whether from wanting to be a boy myself, or having a family who wanted it, I resolved the dilemma of my youth long ago by becoming a tomboy. It was a wonderful solution. Getting out, roaming the hills, walking in the woods, and exploring, which I still do today, was and is all an expression of the same basic need. At bottom, I suppose, it has to do with being unfettered, unrestricted by social definitions of behavior.

In historian Gerder Lerner's book *The Female Experience* I found a moving account of Frances Willard (1839–1898), feminist and temperance leader, and her experience of being a tomboy. In her day she had to undergo the pains of becoming a lady. Lerner's book includes these excerpts from Willard's journals as well as many other women's documents, over half of which were previously unpublished.

Frances Willard, raised with her brothers, was left to roam free with them in the country. When she had to change her ways, she was heartbroken and she wrote:

> No girl went through a harder experience than I, when my free, out-of-door life had to cease, and the long skirts and clubbed-up hair spiked with hair-pins had to be endured. The half of that down-heartedness has never been told and never can be. I always believed that if I had been let alone and allowed as a woman, what I had had as a girl, a free life in the country, where a human being might grow, body and soul, as a tree grows, I would have been "ten times more of a person" every way. Mine was a nature hard to tame, and I cried long and loud when I found I could never again race and range about with freedom. I had delighted in my short hair and nice round hat, or comfortable "Shaker bonnet," but now I was to be "choked with ribbons" when I went into the open air the rest of my days. Something like the following was the "state of mind" that I revealed as a young girl in my journal about this time:
>
> "This is my birthday and the date of my martyrdom. Mother insists that at last I *must* have my hair done up woman-fashion. She says she can hardly forgive herself for letting me run wild so long. We've had a great time over it all, and here I sit like another Samson shorn of my strength. That figure won't do, though, for the greatest trouble with me is that I never shall be shorn again. My "back" hair is twisted up like a corkscrew; I carry eighteen hair-pins; my head aches miserably; my feet are entangled in the skirt of my hateful new gown. I can never jump over a fence again, so long as I live. As for chasing the sheep down in the shady pasture, it's out of the question, and to climb to my eagle's nest seat in the big burr-oak would ruin this new frock beyond repair. Altogether, I recognize the fact that my occupation's gone."

I recognize Willard's childhood feelings as akin to my own. Creating Women in the Wilderness with other women has given me a way to rekindle and live out this occupation, which I call "exploring." For each of us, becoming a woman has had more to do with reclaiming this aspect of herself than eliminating it, as "maturity" did in the past.

This is where support from others is crucial. Society often leaves one feeling very much alone. In knowing and being in touch with other women who share interests, I have come to understand my feelings as normal rather than atypical. Though we roam outside the norm of social ideas of acceptability, we are hardly alone.

We have each taken on a significant and initially terrifying challenge, stretched beyond what we thought we could do, and reached new levels of accomplishment. We've grown, as Frances Willard would say, "as a tree grows."

Many a young life is battered and forever crippled on the breakers of puberty; if it crosses these unharmed and is not dashed to pieces on the rocks of childbirth, it may still run aground on the ever-recurring shallows of menstruation, and lastly upon the final bar of the menopause ere protection is found in the unruffled waters of the harbor beyond reach of sexual storms.

—DR. ENGELMAN,
President of the American Gynecology Society, 1900, in Ehrenreich and English, *For Her Own Good*

IV   Where There Were Friends,
     Where There Were Foes

IV

Where There Were Friends, Where There Were Foes
the wilderness without women, an American dream

at Monaghan, a writer and poet in Alaska, writes to a mutual friend:

> When I was living by myself south of the Salcha for several months I underwent a transformation of which no one had warned me . . . I became something rather terrifying and ugly—to other people. A sort of witch. I went through the same sort of experience that the woman in Margaret Atwood's book *Surfacing* goes through. But there was a reason for the change.
>
> Just before the transformation took place, while I was still in what I call the "Herbal Essence Girl" stage . . . I attracted the notice of construction workers in a camp a couple of miles away. Now I was probably the only woman in the vicinity . . . I dared to live alone and was notably unsociable. Well, one night a bunch of men got drunk and decided to shoot at me, which they did—at least at my cabin. They missed, but I was badly frightened.
>
> I retreated to Anchorage for a few weeks and went into a collapse. But when I returned—against all my friends' advice, I assure you—I knew that something would happen to me. And this is when the transformation into an old hag took place; men rape women, after all, and unprotected women communing with nature sure as hell ought to remember that.
>
> It was an incredible experience; it took place without my noticing it. I was completely ignored by what men I did run into . . . I began to notice, when I happened to catch a glimpse of myself in the door window. I was shocked. I realized that I'd resorted to a very primitive form of self-defense. And believe me, it was effective.
>
> I had actually begun to look about seventy, a phenomenon which my body somehow produced so that I would not be vulnerable. I became like an old witch of the fairy tales who lives outside town and is revealed at night to be a beautiful young woman. She existed, she was I.

At first I ran wild in the forest. I chewed pleasant tasting manzanita berries to allay the pangs of hunger, and once, having fashioned primitive equipment from a stick, some twine, and a bent pin, I actually caught a small fish. I used part of it for bait, but when it became evident that there were no more where that came from, I broiled the remainder on a stick held over a small fire. I felt free, reckless, strangely happy. I bathed in an ice-cold pool at the foot of a small waterfall. The water in the pool was neck-deep, swift as well as cold. It took me off my feet and I didn't know how to swim. Nothing made any difference, nothing frightened me. I hoped I would meet a bear in the woods; I was only shy of people.

—CAROBETH LAIRD,
Encounter with an Angry God

But I also learned something there about the lack of "wildness" in the woods—at least, I learned there is no lack of order, that the order there is perhaps more dangerously unyielding than the order of civilization.

Ever since, I've been spying the trail of that transformation in what other women write about nature. I find traces, too, in mythology. Something happens/can happen to a woman in relation to the wild that has never been really explored.

Pat Monaghan's story sums up a paradox of women in the wilderness. Consciously, society discourages women from going into the wilderness; unconsciously, it associates womanhood and wildness. To explore this apparent contradiction, and to learn more about the connection of woman and wildness, I called on Susan Griffin, author of *Woman and Nature: The Roaring Inside Her.* Following are excerpts from our conversation.

Galland: From your book, it is clear that you understand the association of the two. Some people mention that woman has a special kinship with nature. Others view it as a realm in which she has no place.

Pat Monaghan suggests that there may be a mythic cycle in which one transcends the natural world not by conquering it, but by merging with it. Some people have said that this is particularly natural for women.

Griffin: I don't agree. Men are as capable of merging with nature as women. And women are as capable of conquering and having an attitude of domination as men. It has nothing to do with biology. The archetypes created by our culture are easily confused with more primordial archetypes of the human condition.

I'm writing a book on pornography and I find as I investigate pornographic attitudes throughout culture that our particular culture is hostile to nature and also hostile to women. And the precise element that our culture is hostile to is wildness. Of course, wildness is a part of human nature and we are all afraid of our own wildness—men and women. But what our culture does is to project wildness onto women. We've been the scapegoats for male fear of a quality which is indeed human.

Now I would like to speak on a more personal level about what happens to me when I go into any wildness. Where I walk most frequently is a tame version of wilderness which is the nearby park and nature area, but it's kept relatively unchanged by humans and it's very close to my home. I go there frequently and I find that it's very restoring. It has a similar effect on me as meditation. Every time I go up there I go almost forgetting what the experience is. I say that I want some exercise or fresh air or I just want to be alone with myself for a while. I really feel the effect that that experience has on me because it is of such a different order than one can describe logically. I go up there and I get transformed every time—something incredible happens to me there. I see in a different way. The language that we have is a language of this culture—the nouns we have, the symbols, the reference points, even the grammar is hostile to that kind of experience and this is why many mystics and people who meditate and people who love nature have had such difficulty communicating their experience. Our culture doesn't have any mode to communicate it.

Galland: Do you think that it is specifically our culture or is there something about the nature of the experience itself that is beyond the level of verbal communication?

Griffin: Yes, it is nonverbal, a very sensual experience. It is the ineffable that one is encountering, but in our culture we don't recognize or see this other order of communicating with nature and I don't think that is just accidental.

I think our culture is in fact an expression of the terror and our terrible fear and revenge against nature because we can't accept that we are in fact creatures that are not always in control, we aren't always in logical control. We do things for reasons that we don't know and we don't understand and things happen to us that aren't under our control—hurricanes, death, these things happen to everybody and are not under our control. This is a culture that wants to control.

Galland: Not only does it want to control but it does so desperately.

Griffin: Desperately is a good word. We don't accept our fate. Over and over again, there are Greek dramas and myths that tell us that we as humankind cannot accept our fate. This is the beauty of these myths when we look at them as a key to see what we are doing as a culture. And what is fateful about our lives except nature—our nature— our human nature and the world we live in? I wanted to say physical— but that is a separation—physical/spiritual world we live in—this life is our fate.

Galland: Susan, you've said that the language of our culture only gives us the cerebral realm, but could that just be the nature of language itself?

Griffin: No, I love language and I think language can bring this other realm to us, but this culture's language doesn't. I suspect that in certain tribal cultures there are all kinds of words which evoke this ineffable experience. Of course, nothing can describe the ineffable, but it can be evoked. But our language does not even do that.

Galland: That's quite true. Language has many shapes and forms. I think of chanting, certain kinds of storytelling, the way many Native Americans speak is very evocative.

I'm drawn deeper and deeper into stillness. Once I was always afraid of the dark—and I would go a few paces out into the moonless nights of sound and then quickly turn around and come back.

Now, I take long quiet walks all alone on the darkest nights to sit on boulders where the water is fast and white—or go searching the woods for luminescent wood fungi that glow in the dark with an eerie color.

I have made friends with the night.
—JANE BYRD

The eucalyptus shimmering in the fog is speaking to me. It never occurred to me until this moment that the tree that catches my eye in the early evening fog does so for a purpose. Yet the tree is just one of several in a stand of eucalyptus. This one alone shimmers green-silver in the light.

I presume. Perhaps I am merely allowed to observe a moment in the tree's life, a moment of fullness and radiance. Perhaps it has just had a great illumination and I can stand there for a moment in its uncanny light. Or do I have the moment of illumination and so can see the tree illumined; or do the tree and I merge, tall, peeling, silver-barked, wet-leafed and all?

—CHINA GALLAND

The return to the green chaos, the deep forest and the refuge of the unconcious . . . is essential to the human mind. Without it, it disintegrates and we go mad.

—JOHN FOWLES,
"On Seeing Nature Whole,"
Harpers, November 1979

Griffin: Yes, they have a phrase—"spirit world"—and it means something quite different than what we mean when we say heaven, which we don't believe in anymore. The spirit world is always existing—the spirit world isn't something that you go up or down to—it exists right along with you.

Galland: One of the important things about your book *Woman and Nature* was the way in which you used language.

Griffin: The method of knowing that the kind of language in that book is built around is similar to the French poet's statement "The ultimate proof of water is thirst." It's poetic logic and that's also the logic of wildness. If you think about all the reverberations of that statement, it's ultimately a very trusting philosophy—it seems that you are trusting the universe. And there isn't something wrong with you in your essential nature that creates a tragedy. It means that the universe is kind to your nature, that the universe provides for your nature.

Galland: Which brings us back again to the association of women, nature, and wildness.

Griffin: Associatively, we have many Western male thinkers who have been able to go so far as to say that wildness in people is something that ought to be looked at again because it may be the source of all creativity. James Hillman says that in the sense that he talks about the libido and the erotic nature of creativity and the fact that the dream world and the unconscious mind is not just a body of repressed material waiting to be censored—but represents another way of thinking that is very rich. Many thinkers since Freud will say in one way or another that culture and nature don't have to be at war. That's one of Freud's basic premises.

But as this psychoanalytic debate goes on, many have been able to see the connection between culture and nature, but they can't see the link between nature and women. They fail to understand that the fear and hatred and denigration of women is the same thing as the fear of nature. That the denigration of wildness in human nature, which is also the libido, the sexual part, is also a denial of a part of the self that is creative. The same feelings of danger that this civilization holds toward sexuality and instincts, wild animals and wild nature, is the same feeling of danger they hold toward women. The fear of women being powerful, the fear of wildness, the all-powerful divine mother, it's the same thing. So it is possible for a culture, it is possible for a human being, in this civilization to be able to recognize that nature is not the enemy, but they may still not be able to make the link that woman is not the enemy either.

On one level of causality, I think the reason that culture developed in a way that is hostile to nature and to women has to do with the human condition, the vulnerability of infants. It is not accidental that hostility would get focused on women since the mother represents nature to the child. However, the decision to invent a culture which denied and took vengeance on both women and nature was not inevitable. I myself believe there were earlier cultures that didn't make that decision. That's my belief—I know it can't be proven. I myself also, in all the looking that I have done at tribal cultures, believe that there were and even still are many cultures, for instance the Native American cultures, that are far less hostile to women and far less hostile to nature. I know there are anthropologists that don't believe that about Native American culture, but I myself am much more skeptical of words I hear from anthropologists than I am of words I hear from Indians.

Galland: When you say that, I think of the Native American traditions, many of which honor the female and nature. What has happened in our society is not inevitable, I agree. At least this is my understanding from talking with Native Americans, though not from anthropology.

Griffin: Anyone who looks more deeply at anthropological methods knows that, half the time, an anthropologist goes somewhere and the person who is supposedly an informant is putting them on. On top of that, as we all do, they filter in what they have learned through their own screen. Half of the people in the nineteenth century who looked at Indians (which was before we destroyed those cultures) would never have looked for female equality. If they heard of a deity, they would assume it was a man. If they saw a form of power that a woman was exercising, they would assume that it was not really powerful because she was a woman. So there is a stance that even very politically astute white scientists take, of superiority toward other peoples, that is very hard to break through. There is an assumption that because they are scientists and the other person is the object of their study that they can describe that person's life better than the person himself. There is something wrong with that.

Galland: Susan, when we first met I mentioned the link that I sense is important to make between the women's movement and the environmental movement. You agreed, yet many people find this bridge difficult to understand. How would you describe its significance?

Griffin: The best example of why I think they ought to be linked is the fact that Stewart Brand and other people in the ecology movement who work very hard and who certainly are to be recognized as very legitimate spokesmen for the environmental movement, came out in favor of space colonies as a solution to the destruction of the biosphere. When I first read that I was amazed that "environmentalists" would

Wildness is the state of complete awareness.

—KRISHNAMURTI,
in Dolores La Chapelle,
Earth Wisdom

IN THE OXFORD ENGLISH
DICTIONARY ONE READS:

*That the word "woman" is a
formation peculiar to English which
did not appear until the late
thirteenth century. Until then the
word for woman had been "wife."*

*That the word "wild" comes from
the Welsh,* gwyllt, *and the Irish,*
geilt, *in the eighth century, and
means living in a state of nature,
not tame, not domesticated, not
cultivated, uncivilized, savage,
uncultured, rude, rebellious, not
under control, unconfined, or
unrestricted, unruly, restive, reckless,
careless, irregular, erratic, unsteady,
insubordinate, wayward, dissolute,
loose, fierce, furious, violent, stormy,
tempestuous, full of disturbance,
tumultuous, turbulent, highly
excited, passionately vehement,
demented, unreasonable, resisting
control, resisting restraint, at
random, astray.*

*That "wilderness" came into the
language around the twelfth century
and means a wild or uncultivated
tract of land, uninhabited or
inhabited only by wild animals, or
a piece of ground in a large garden
or park, planted with trees and laid
out in a fantastic style, often in the
form of a maze or labyrinth.*

*That "manly" means human.
Possessing the virtues proper to a man
as distinguished from a woman or
child; chiefly, courageous,
independent in spirit, frank, upright.*

*That "womanly" means having
the qualities (as of gentleness,
devotion, fearfulness, etc.)
characteristic of women.*

think of leaving the earth and being in a colony, it astonished me—I
became speechless. I suppose that after I got over my initial amazement
it seemed predictable because unless you can understand psychologically
what is at the very origin of the fear and hatred of nature, you can't
make the connection. The ecology movement is going to make the same
mistake that Western society made in the first place unless it understands
this.

Galland: Could we say that the mistake lies in fearing and hating
that which we can't control? Not only do we fear and attempt to control
what we perceive as "other," but we compound our error by imagining
that "it," whether it is woman or nature, is separate and incidental to
us. This seems to be the common ground of the error in societal attitudes
toward both women and the environment.

Griffin: It's exactly the attitude that this civilization takes toward the
earth—and the ecology movement is in danger if it doesn't understand
more fundamentally why these attitudes have evolved and how they
are linked to a fear of the feminine. The ecology movement is in danger
of imitating it, in the same way the American radical left has in many
ways imitated the basic lack of concern for life and for other human
beings that the main culture itself lacks. There are some exceptions to
that statement that we all revere, like Martin Luther King. I think that
in addition to the repression from the government the radical left has
defeated itself because it hasn't had a reverence for the other, and for
life itself.

I heard another leader in the environmental movement comment not
long ago about a starving nation. His position was that we should let
them starve because if we feed them the population will just continue
to expand.

This is the kind of thinking that falls under the category of
quantification—you reduce people to numbers. If we feed them this
11,000 will turn into 12,000 and they would say that is "hard thinking"
as opposed to "soft-mindedness" and soft-mindedness would be the
female reaction. But how can you let a baby starve? That kind of thinking
is natural, that is nature. And that is what I want to preserve in the
ecology movement. I don't want to survive in a world that thinks of a
baby, a single human baby, as expendable. That's not survival to me.
I'm not just talking about my flesh surviving—I'm talking about my
heart surviving which is flesh and spirit and everything. I want all of
that to survive.

After our talk I sit and think about wildness and why we can find
it threatening. Wildness is forever growing through the cracks in the
cement, having to be mowed, paved over, cut back, trimmed, fenced.

It erupts, shifts, surfaces, flows. For this we explain, reason, plan, forecast, predict, anything to cover up our fear, to avoid our vulnerability in the face of this eternal changing, which can take us over, cover us again with forests and with trees, fill us with animals, cats that growl deep in the night. We cannot see but we hear the horned owl hoot nearby; a deer crashes through the underbrush. The old order reemerges.

Joy Hardin sends me a chapter of the late Dawn Gherman's work, entitled "From Civilization to Savage, the Idea of Feminine Wildness." It's a study of the standard female figure in American literature of the frontier. She is generally portrayed as reluctant to leave civilization, dreading the wilderness and fearing Indians. Much of the material examined comes from the frontier days of the nineteenth century, yet this image is more persistent than one would like to think and isn't just confined to American literature.

Dawn Gherman's doctoral study *From Parlour to Tepee: The White Squaw on the American Frontier* examines this image and contrasts it with material actually written by women of the frontier. Her work suggests a different kind of woman from those portrayed by male authors and critics. In her preface she explains that her study grew out of the conflict she had found between her "self-image as a white woman and a culturally-defined image which I have repeatedly confronted." The conflict is reflected in differences between the way women recorded their frontier experience and the way men depicted them. There is often a wide discrepancy.

I recognize the conflict she describes and I am drawn to her pursuit of feminine wildness. She defines it as "the propensity to break social taboos which restrict self-expression and exploration." She describes the wilderness taboo as the implicit social assumption that white women can't go into the wilderness. She sees the taboo as a psychological limit against entering the wilderness, an activity which helps develop behavior that may conflict with the roles fostered by society.

I know from my own experience what she's talking about. Once outside a circle of like-minded friends, there is a subtle and pervasive discouragement that still exists.

One summer I went with my family on a canoe trip into the sloughs and bayous of east Texas. It was a pleasant, easy weekend experience with husband and children together. Two weeks later I went back to do the same trip with only my friend Hope Shaw, and in glaring contrast, at every filling station or food stop where people noticed the canoe on top of the car, we were warned of danger: alligators and bears, snakes dropping out of trees, and the likelihood of our getting completely lost in the steamy bayous. By the time we arrived at our campground, the situation was comical. As we paid our fee, the park ranger warned us that if we walked around at night we would be bitten by rattlesnakes,

How limited we become by all that is untried and unexplored within us! How can I surmount my further limits if I have not pushed through the boundaries of those closer at hand?

—BARBARA HAZILLA

and what were we doing "going camping alone anyway?" Being with another woman constituted being alone. That did it. We put aside all fears, set up camp, and went canoeing. We never saw the rattlesnakes, bears, or alligators or had a snake drop onto us out of a tree. And we still laugh about what a good time we had "alone." There is support available from both women and men, if you seek it out, to counter the general societal discouragement of women who want to get outside.

In her study, Gherman points out that, like many before them, the Puritans historically viewed the wilderness as the place of the devil and its inhabitants as his followers. Indians were often referred to as demons or devils, or thought to be in desperate need of conversion. And it followed that since woman's place is in the home, the woman in the wilderness was a threat to the social order. In the frontier tradition, she claims, the entry of the white woman, the civilizer, brought the expulsion from Eden, the end of the white man's American wilderness, his exclusive domain. There are traces of this attitude today.

As though to document Gherman's premise, we receive in the Women in the Wilderness office an article titled "The Computer Labored and Brought Forth a Bear," which appeared in the January, 1978, *TV Guide*. Oddly revealing, the subject is *Grizzly Adams*, a television series produced by millionaire Charles Sellier, who believes that "God wants me to do the kind of films that I do, otherwise he wouldn't have made me a success."

Sellier's success has come through developing sophisticated computer programs based on audience preferences from all over the country that predict typical audience reactions to a TV show. The show *Grizzly Adams* is a construct of computer-tested likes and dislikes.

The results of Sellier's tests showed that the American public "likes waterfalls, pretty vistas, and high mountain ridges, preferably with actors and animals as part of the scene. They dislike snow except at Christmas." From these surveys, he devised the character of Grizzly Adams, a bearded mountain man of the 1850s who befriends a lovable grizzly bear. Apparently Sellier discovered that grizzlies with long claws are a favorite of the American audience along with otters, chipmunks, and burros. There were no female characters in the show.

When women executives at NBC objected to the lack of any female role in the series, Sellier created an episode called "Woman in the Wilderness," "against my better judgment," he said. After running it through his computerized audience response program, Sellier canned the episode: audience response from the computer was negative. "I proved my point, but it was expensive," he commented later. "What the American public likes is eternal summer in the primeval womanless wilderness." That may indeed be the twentieth-century TV viewer's preference, but Gherman's sources indicated that many women enjoyed frontier life, had a love of the landscape, and relished the greater flexibility in social roles. Some enjoyed their life alongside the Indians. Life in the wilderness was then and still can be a refuge from socially assigned roles.

Much of Gherman's work contradicts stereotypical traditional images of Indians as well as of women in frontier literature. Indians, in accounts written by frontier women, were described as "kind" and "loving," though "fierce towards their foes." White captives were sometimes adopted into Indian families. Some captives chose never to return to the world of white civilization, though they were often given the opportunity. Mary Jemison, a captive who stayed with her adopted tribe and took Indian husbands, had several children and owned her own land at a time when married white women were forbidden to own property.

The literature of those days, as recorded by traditional scholars and historians, fails to convey the frontier experience from a woman's point of view. Gherman's work also brings to light how women ran farms, drove mule teams, protected settlements, traded with trappers, miners, and the Indians.

Occasionally these women married and lived with the Indians on their own. The Indian women themselves had developed a wisdom about the wilderness that was unknown to white women; and there are many instances of their sharing their knowledge. Black women were present on the frontier too. One was Billie Mason, who crossed the continent on foot with her daughter and established her own homestead in California in the 1860s.

Gherman's research was supported by a Woodrow Wilson Fellowship. Her ideas and her extensive bibliography beg for further exploration. Though much of her study is historical, its relationship to contemporary women's experiences, mine and others', is interesting, since even today we find ourselves often being discouraged from going off into the wilderness by dire warnings of its dangers and hardships.

Before Irene Miller's historic climb, her daughters were told that their mother was crazy. Irene was one of the two women who made it to the summit of Annapurna in 1978 on the American Women's Himalayan Expedition. People consider men who climb mountains "heroic," "daring," and "admirable," but a woman who does the same thing is often still regarded as a deviant. And, though there is much talk of liberation on both sides, the depth to which our sex roles are ingrained and the extent to which they inhibit our connection to wilderness, and our free enjoyment of it, is remarkable.

When white persons of either sex have been taken prisoners young by the Indians, and lived a while among them, tho ransomed by their Friends, and treated with all imaginable tenderness to prevail with them to stay among the English, yet in a short time they become disgusted with our manner of life, and the care and pains that are necessary to support it and take the first good opportunity of escaping again into the Woods, from whence there is no reclaiming them.

—BENJAMIN FRANKLIN, 1753

V   The Pattern of the Winds

V

The Pattern of the Winds
contemporary women adventurers, a look at a new heroic for women

he traditional concept of the hero is a dangerous notion: someone, usually male, will come along and single-handedly save the world. The movie *Superman*, in which the hero literally moves mountains, holds together the Hoover Dam, and backs up the Colorado River, accurately depicts this fantasy. I watched it on a cross-country flight without the earphones. The dialogue was irrelevant; we all know the story. Superman saves the world and the girl he loves, then, in a last show of self-sacrifice, gives her up and flies off into the sunset.

All in good fun, or is it? Unfortunately many of us interpret stories like this as evidence that someone else will save the world, the country, the environment, or our souls. This kind of fantasy leaves us in an existential limbo, waiting for someone else to accomplish the task at hand. It is also uncomfortably close to what I was taught as a young woman: that a man, presumably a husband, would provide all the necessities for my existence and for the existence of any children we might have. Many of us know what a mistaken idea that has been. But this malady of wanting someone else to live life for us affects both women and men. We all have days when we want to forget that we are completely responsible for ourselves. The upbringing that many women have had is just a further distortion of a basic human delusion; someone else will do it for you.

The part that is true about a mythical figure such as Superman is that we are all capable of much more than we know. Stories of heroes reveal our heights and depths. Nevertheless, I find it problematic that the most widely known hero stories are expressions of only one kind of experience of the world. The word "hero" itself is unsatisfactory, but "heroine," the feminine form, is diminutive. However, we all have some common understanding of the term heroic.

Discovering what is heroic for women, going on the premise that women's experience of the world is distinctly different from that of

The real leader has no need to lead—[s]he is content to point the way. Unless we become our own leaders, content to be what we are in the process of becoming, we shall always be servitors and idolators.
—HENRY MILLER,
The Wisdom of the Heart

Women Outward Bound instructors had also been thinking along these lines; two came as participants in the course.

Clare Rhoades and Anne Ketchin received a modicum of financial and office support from Outward Bound International to consult on developing women's courses in the various O.B. schools around the country.

men, means charting unexplored waters. As I said earlier, the issue is epistemological rather than sexual. Women have a different mode of perception. Because much of women's experience has not been documented, but has been lost or stricken from the record as valueless, we have no genuinely female concept of the heroic. Such a concept would help us value ourselves. No one is going to do that for us, nor will anyone value us *until* we do this for ourselves. We are only now beginning to talk about the quality of our own experience as women rather than defining ourselves or being defined as being whatever is opposite of male.

My own explorations of this line of thought began as a hunch I had years ago after an abbreviated Outward Bound course. I was emboldened by what I discovered I could do. I wanted to do more. I assumed that there had to be other women like myself with work and family who needed to be outdoors. I put together the first Adult Women's Outward Bound course that fall, 1974. We spent a week rafting and hiking along the Rio Grande in Texas, along the Mexican border. It was a success. Women wanted more. Now women's trips are offered by virtually all the Outward Bound schools in the United States.

Most of our ideas about what is heroic arise from one-sided descriptions of experience that we find embedded in the classic Western stories of the heroic journey. This came to me clearly when I was in the process of designing a university course around the notion of the heroic quest in 1975, after I had moved to California. We were to combine a study of the classic Western myths with our own journey into the wilderness. I began to think about the classical myths of the *Iliad*, the *Odyssey*, the *Aeneid, Beowulf*, King Arthur and the Knights of the Round Table. All the heroes were men. The women in the stories were extraneous characters. Helen of Troy was a political pawn. Circe turned men into pigs. Penelope was the model of a faithful wife, for twenty long years. The great queen Dido, after founding Carthage, tossed herself onto a funeral pyre when Aeneas set sail. There were no women at the Round Table, and the strongest female character in *Beowulf* that came to mind was a monster, Grendel's mother. I vaguely recalled Joan of Arc, but her life was unfortunately brief. The more I thought about the course, the less enthusiastic I became. So I organized a backpacking weekend for women instead and began questioning others on this subject. Who do we as women use for models? What qualities do we admire, aspire to? Is there such a thing as "the heroic" for women? And, since we're all human, what parts of the classical stories still hold and are true of the human psyche, regardless of sex?

Joseph Campbell, in his classic work *Hero with a Thousand Faces*, describes the elements common to all the quest stories; these he calls the monomyth. It seems evident that the myths offer us a diagram for becoming whole and confirm the key experiences which we can expect to encounter in such a process. These are some of the features Campbell outlines in the traditional heroic quest stories: there is a departure in which the hero, representing everyone, sets out upon a journey, and an encounter with the guardian of the other world—the unknown, the unconscious. There is often a meeting with the mother goddess; an atonement with the father; a sacred marriage; and the winning of the boon, a gift, the elixir of life, which is symbolized in the myths as the grail cup or the golden fleece, for example. In truth, the prize is wholeness and the realization that, as Campbell says, the world of the gods is but a forgotten dimension of the world we know. The prize is won, and now Everyone, the hero, must return. The journey back can be equally perilous and is fraught with danger. The ultimate test is the return to the community and the integration back into everyday life.

Campbell's summary, though helpful, also illuminates some of the difficulty women may have with the notion of "heroic." We have so often linked heroism with warfare, battling, conquest, and victory that a different notion of heroism, one that allows us to see nurturing and sustaining as heroic activities, is difficult to develop. Yet this is what must be done. We need to value actions in which one identifies with rather than opposes another being or way of being. The idea of battling and fighting is only one of the ways of dealing with fear, conflict, and difference. Often that which we reject and oppose is the very person or position that we need to include within our embrace.

Acceptance is the art of making the obstacle the path. Therefore, embrace the enemy. This is the lesson of the river guide: face the danger, move toward it, that's where the current is the strongest, and it will carry you around the obstacle. Use it. In Aikido, a Japanese martial art, our teacher would say, blend, never turn from your attackers, move right in next to them, see the world from their point of view. Identify with the enemy and they are transformed. Opponents are lively, giving you energy: accept the gift. These ideas are not passive: taken from Aikido, from Zen, from the river, they demand an alertness and ability to respond that are complete. Our first task is to become the leaders of our own lives, heroes of our own stories. In fact, we already are; we have only to discover what that means.

Each of the classical stories singles out an individual hero, yet in every case that hero is assisted by friendly powers. Without intervention from outside, the hero would fail. An alternative view of heroism would focus on the entire complex, the context in which the hero completes the task, seeing all the helpers along the way as also accomplishing the heroic work. For in truth heroic matters require all of us giving our best, contributing our part. No one is saved alone. Our task remains the same today as in the old stories: saving the community, redeeming the world. The very nature of such a task transcends individual concerns, and yet somehow the task is only accomplished through the individual and within the web of community. The mystery is that we must all save each other but can do so only by becoming ourselves. No one is saved until we are all saved. The Bodhisattva of the Buddhist tradition, which I now study, gives me a clue, points a new direction.

The Bodhisattva, the enlightened being, Avalokitesvara, is depicted as androgynous in many cases. There is also a female form of the Bodhisattva called Kwan Yin in Chinese. Kwan Yin, "the hearer of the world's cries," has as her greatest virtue compassion—"compassion" from the Latin meaning to feel with. In Tibet one finds the female Buddha Tara, beloved by the people. In Tibetan the word "Bodhisattva" is itself translated as "heroic being."

Compassion, redeeming the community, are clues. Another clue is the importance of courage. It is an essential quality, but I think we've often interpreted it wrongly. Being courageous doesn't mean being without fear. Courage acknowledges and includes fear. It means being willing to live with fear rather than deny or reject it. This demands a certain magnitude of heart. In Buddhism, too, courage is a central virtue, close to the heart of the matter, the matter being your life.

Long ago I discovered that my fear was often an indication of what I had to do next. Whatever I was most afraid of would often come about, unless I learned to include the object of my fear in my life. The more experiences I have outdoors, the more I come to understand fear, learn how to work with it and use it. Here is where I have found the wilderness particularly rich, because confronting my fears there affords me a way to experiment with my life, to try out different ways of using it. Often women are taught to withdraw when fear arises; whereas men are taught that taking risks can bring high gains, and so tend to ignore the feelings. Neither sex has developed a very appropriate reponse, withdrawing or ignoring. There must be another way.

I run a day-long workshop for a women's group on demystifying fear. We begin the day with a silent morning walk through a nearby woods. The air is cool on my cheeks, light flickers through the windblown trees. The electric green of new growth is startling against the darkness of winter branches.

Arriving in a clearing, we sit and begin to talk about fear. It has positive aspects. The normal physical sensation of fear signals us to be alert, to pay attention or watch for danger. But there comes a moment in the experience when it becomes critical to move through the fear, or we become lost in it.

We begin to play games designed to help people feel their physical center of balance, to become aware of their connection with the earth.

We form a circle. Rosalie Moore stands in the middle, closes her eyes, and falls backward into another woman's arms. We pass her around the circle, still falling, back and forth, her feet keeping the center. She is thinking, "Will they drop me? Can they bear my weight?" When the circle is done, she opens her eyes, which are moist with excitement.

The next activity is similar, but the fall is from a height. We line up two by two below the crotch of an old redwood tree, with our arms crossed firefighter's fashion to catch the one who will fall backward into our arms. I ask Jane to stand in the crotch of the tree with her back to us. She has a marked curvature of the spine and her back is a particularly vulnerable place. Now I am asking her to fall on it. She climbs up into the crotch and stands there breathless, unable to imagine how she can ever do it. Though she is only four feet off the ground, her fear is great. It's not the height, it's the moment of letting go that is terrifying.

Her breath shortens, her throat tightens. She rocks back and forth on the balls of her feet, and each time she begins to let herself fall, she stops, grabbing the tree. The tension grows. We say, "Trust." She knows that she has to trust us, but her body and mind are locked in battle. "Breathe," I tell her, "just keep breathing." We often forget to breathe and anxiety skyrockets. She takes a deep breath, then another, and another, yells, "Here I come!" and lets go, toppling into everyone's arms below. For that instant she is out of control and surrendering to the fifteen women in whose arms she lies. They begin to rock her gently as she catches her breath in their arms. Then tears come, the tears of relief, tears of release, the tears that soften the hardness and wear down the stone corners. She breaks through to the other side.

Not long after the workshop, I get together with Rosalie Moore. Rosalie is the only black woman I know who's involved in rafting, backpacking, and outdoor activities. Not only do I like her personally after meeting her in the workshop, but I am curious about her because she is black. I am awkward calling her up and telling her so, but it is important to me. In the wilderness and in the environmental movement, I look around and see white faces, rarely black, brown, or Native American.

Rosalie Moore rappelling

She agrees to see me and we sit and talk one afternoon about her love of the outdoors: "I feel alone quite often; my path is a particularly individual one. . . . I know that I'm one of the few black people you've seen in the wilderness and that's how I feel too. I have to stop and ask myself from time to time, How come I've made my life away from other black people? How come I do things where I'm the only one around? Often I think color is unimportant, that we're all beyond that, and then I go to a meeting and I'm the only black there. That stands out. Then there's the other side of that coin, and that's going to a meeting and finding another black person there and I catch myself thinking, 'Hey, I didn't give you permission to come.' Gradually I've become more aware of how some of the aloneness that I encounter is self-created. And then some of it just comes from following my own particular path, like going into the wilderness. That's just plain me."

Rosalie began getting out into the countryside with her family when she was a child. "I was just an outdoor spirit. There was something in me that never could fit in the city. I have no idea where or why." She and her sister were Girl Scouts and had early camping experiences together with their mother, which she recalls warmly now. And then there was her grandmother Nana, tall, strong, and thin. Nana raised her family alone from the time she was twenty-three, when her husband died. "She never did anything like climb Annapurna, but you knew she could have. She had that kind of strength," Rosalie tells me.

I too had a grandmother named Nana with whom I am still connected, even after her death. Grandmothers, old women who have gone before, survivors leaving us their heritage, are heroes to us now. Rosalie shares these feelings, making a place where friendship can grow.

By the end of our visit, her blackness is inconsequential, Rosalie as a person is so large. I am inspired by her patience and her willingness to follow her own mind, whether she has companions or not. This is a kind of private heroism, taking on everyone's demons about color and not being deflected from her own path. You'll never read about such courage in the paper, but this is where it all begins, in your own backyard.

Private heroism, acts of courage that do not show: our lives are filled with them. I think of Laree Zierk, a fifty-one-year-old grandmother who came down the Grand Canyon with me. She did not swim, and yet traveled 226 miles through the rapids downriver hardly mentioning that fact. She had been married nearly all her adult life, raised a family, found herself divorced in her late forties and very much alone. One morning on the river she read to us from Anne Lindbergh's *Gift from the Sea* on solitude, not as meaning being alone, but as a means of uniting oneself with the sacred core in the center of being. As she read, her eyes filled with tears, and I recognized the great loneliness she had gone through, beyond, into the wellspring found only in solitude. I could see that it had not been easy.

She wrote to me later about our experience. "There are still difficulties in my life, but 'this woman has survived Lava Falls.' That inner strength is still there to draw upon, and that is what is most important."

Starting over again, she met difficulty with a quiet, admirable strength and gracefulness that I admire.

I continue to explore the question of the heroic and women, this time in the *Women in the Wilderness* quarterly. In response to a query published there, I received a letter from Ann Stewart, a member in Sacramento. In it she related how she organized an "Adventure Series for Women" through the local YWCA. Thirty-five women came together and listed all the activities they had always wanted to try but never had out of fear or lack of opportunity.

Twelve members of the group had never slept outside on the ground before. They went rafting, though none had ever been in a raft. The river trip was so successful that afterward two of the forty-year-old members went on to become river guides. Throughout the year, they continued with a variety of activities: rock climbing, scuba diving, caving, sailing, horseback riding, just to mention a few. "It was a very valuable, nonthreatening way to have these experiences," Ann writes.

And yet she too is puzzled by the question "What is heroic for women?" She thinks of Harriet Tubman, leading slaves into freedom, or Ann Davison, who sailed by herself across the Atlantic. Then she mentions a friend, left to raise four children alone. Recently, with great trepidation, this friend purchased her own boat and is teaching herself to sail. "Is she any less heroic than the women who climbed Annapurna?" Ann Stewart asks.

When I arrive at Susan Griffin's with this question, a woman carpenter opens the door and shows me outside, where Susan and I are to sit overlooking the backyard edged with pine. In the middle stands a peach tree, soft and heavy with fruit.

"We don't give recognition to someone who does heroic things along the lines of what is considered feminine work," Susan responds. "Whoever invented the wheel? What a brilliant invention that was! What about the person who invented the pot?" The way the heroic is talked about now, she maintains, always has something to do with power, "That kind of power over people, not the kind of power that someone has when they have a natural power in them. The power of truth empowers others, like the power of music, or image, or emotional perception."

Susan mentions raising children, too. "I don't mean to be sentimental the way some people can be about raising children, but there is something heroic in raising a child, and it's not what men think, and yes, it is heroic. There is a herculean labor involved here that isn't recognized at all. Such work is never recognized, never used. No one tells that story, passing on this knowledge of ours and making it into a greater part of how we live. Women know so much about human beings. . . . We raise them and our wisdom is ignored."

The talk with Susan gives me another clue. What women have done that's heroic has been ignored, by society and by women within it. Here's the task: coming to value ourselves and that realm of work and experience that the world ignores. This may be the heroic task for every woman: maintaining the value of our experience in the face of a world that not only ignores but is hostile to the qualities of nurturing and sustenance that we stand for.

Nancy Jack Todd sends me her thoughts on the subject of the heroic. A founder and co-director of the New Alchemy Institute, Nancy has become well known for her contributions to the institute's researches in environmentally harmonious gardening, aquaculture, and energy production.

"When I think of the heroic, the first image that swims into my mind is one from the classic period of heroes. It is one of splendid, bronzed youths, clasping shields, restraining rearing horses with nostrils flared— all valorous and beautiful, stereotypical and remote, touching my own life only through movies or the dimly remembered cover of my Latin textbook.

"The second image that comes to me, following swiftly and completely eradicating the first, moves me a great deal more. It is a photograph from the book *The Family of Man*, the photographs collected by Edward Steichen for the Museum of Modern Art. I first saw it long before I had children of my own, and one photograph has stayed with me since, embodying for me qualities as heroic as those classical warriors. The photograph is of a black woman, probably young, but seemingly ageless. She stands against a wall, outside, almost in silhouette. She is very thin, slightly swaybacked, and absolutely flat-chested. On her head is a kerchief and she is wearing a skimpy, much-washed sweater and a kilt. She has her children, a girl and a boy, on either side of her. She holds the boy, who is older, lightly against her. The little girl, whose face is completely shadowed, stands next to her leg. The woman's face is inscrutable, partly because of the shadow, but more because she wishes to reveal nothing. The caption reads, 'She is a tree of life to them.' For me, the strength of that woman is absolute. She stands unmoved, constant in her vigilance for her children. She is untouched by the curiosity of the camera, undefeated by her obvious poverty and the hardness of her life.

"Shifting from the ephemeral world of imagery to people I have known, there are quite a few who have done admirable and demanding things: scaled mountains, crossed the sea alone, had harrowing escapes. Of these, the one with the most heroic quality is a woman. She is now over seventy. She is Jewish. With the exception of her husband and her son, all her closest family died in Nazi concentration camps. She fled occupied Europe in the early forties, taking her young son with her. I realize that such incidents are not rare, and that many have involved great bravery, but it is less my friend's past that causes me to catch my breath than the wholeness of spirit that remains with her.

She has never tried to repress her pain or her loss, yet as a teacher, she meets each student, child and adult, as a particularly wonderful and unique discovery. She has let those she lost live still by loving them in other children and other friends. Rather than live out a bitter and alienated old age, she is, in our community, a major source of genuine culture, and of joy. She stands less than five feet in height, yet the only adequate description of her is in E. E. Cummings's words, 'Spirit colossal (& daunted by always nothing).'

"As I continue to pursue thoughts of womanhood and the heroic, I remember Judith Jamison dancing 'Cry.' She sweeps onto the stage, immensely tall, always in motion. A very long scarf billows behind and around her as she dances. She is unbelievably elegant. A few moments later, with a change of sequence, she is on her knees on the stage, the clouds of scarf crumpled into a rag with which she mops the floor. Every vertebra in her back portrays the weariness of endless, unrewarded drudgery, the anonymity of countless lives. Then, later, she is on her feet again. The music is jazz, and she is a temptress, sensual, wild with energy, completely untamable. The dance is dedicated to all black women, and in Jamison's dancing their heroism is unmistakable.

"As perpetrators, but not, in the main, the creators of culture, and as women, we have let the transcendent, masculine idea of the heroic continue, without challenge or redefinition. In the minds of most people it involves rather singular feats most usually performed by a male, which, except in cases of daring rescue, normally implies some sense of conquest; of mountains or seas, enemies or wild beasts, and now of space. It is the male, triumphant, that is most often understood as symbolizing the heroic, but the young women who, throughout all of human experience, have been dispatched through marriage from family and often native language and culture to neighboring tribes, villages, and nations with the mission of maintaining peaceful relations have gone largely unacknowledged, however demanding and long-lasting their tasks. The enduring, the comforting, the sustaining, and the discipline to bring a particular attentiveness to the daily demands of life takes a very powerful kind of courage. And when what is unrecognized and often painfully routine is done with a quality of joy, it becomes heartfelt as was understood in the archaic meaning of the word 'courage.' This kind of heroism is common in the lives of women.

"Now, as we move into a time in which all humanity is challenged to survive and to protect the earth, it may be that women will find themselves confronted with the possibilities for expanded heroism. In the past two decades, through political mobilization, we have been instrumental in ending the Vietnam War, in banning the hydrogen bomb, and in achieving the limitation on nuclear testing. With events continuing to escalate terrifyingly in both political and ecological spheres so that it is not exaggerated to say that almost all life is threatened, I feel that we are challenged to a desperate effort to try to stave off the ultimate nightmare. In becoming embattled in such a struggle, there needs to be a reenvisioning of the heroic from an ideal of splendidly risking death to one of valuing the stubborn courage necessary to see that life goes on."

AWHE PARTICIPANTS

ARLENE BLUM, expedition leader, 10 expeditions in Asia and Africa, including 1976 American Bicentennial Everest Expedition; deputy leader, first all-woman ascent of Mount McKinley; biochemist investigating environmental chemicals, University of California, Berkeley.

JOAN FIREY, food coordinator; veteran Pacific Northwest climber with many first ascents; physical therapist in orthopedics and sport medicine; commercial artist specializing in mountain portraits, Seattle, Washington.

ALISON CHADWICK-ONYSZKIEWICZ, expeditions in Hindu Kush (Noshaq 24,500 feet) and Karakorum; first ascent of Gasherbrum III, 26,200 feet. Art lecturer. Deceased.

LIZ KLOBUSICKY, European equipment; numerous technical ascents of rock and ice routes in the Alps; northwest face of Half Dome, Yosemite; English lecturer from Spokane, Washington, presently living in Germany.

VERA KOMARKOVA, communications; new face route, Mount Dickey, Alaska; all-woman ascent of Mount McKinley; plant ecologist, doing research in Alaskan tundra, Boulder, Colorado.

Taking on one's own fears, befriending them, learning to know the wind, decipher the weather, read the rapids, raise children, all are large tasks. Perhaps the only distinction between these private encounters with fear and the sort of public encounter which the American Women's Himalayan Expedition (AWHE) made is just that, one is public and one is private. What we have called heroic may just be what's visible. A dramatic undertaking such as the climb may become known to many people, but who can say which act requires more courage? Much heroism is ongoing and private, interior and unseen. Perhaps the best of it, like the best charity, is anonymous. The effect is there, untraceable to a single source.

Still, the AWHE Annapurna climb stands out in the imaginations of many women and crops up in conversations on the subject. To learn more about that experience, I call on Arlene Blum, who organized the American Women's Himalayan Expedition, which reached the summit of Annapurna on October 15, 1978.

We sit on the back porch of her house in Berkeley discussing the expedition. She is recovering from a recent illness. Now, as when we've talked before, her modesty about her accomplishments disarms me.

Arlene was a member of the 1978 Bicentennial Everest Expedition and had done all-women climbs of Mount McKinley in Alaska and the Pamirs in Russia before organizing the Annapurna expedition. I am struck by the thought that the climb may have done more to advance the cause of women's rights than the lengthy battle for the Equal Rights Amendment. Ironically, Blum is not a feminist except by coincidence. Liberation, like happiness, is a by-product, not something to be aimed for directly. A Ph.D. in chemistry, Blum likes to climb and has pursued her interest fully.

Two of her fellow climbers, Irene Miller and Vera Komarkova, and their sherpas, Mingma Tshermg and Chewang Rinzi, reached the 26,245-foot summit on October 15, 1978. Two days later, while making a second attempt at the summit, two of the climbers, Vera Watson and Alison Chadwick, plunged two thousand feet to their death. At home, I followed Irene Miller's and Vera Komarkova's progress to the top and attended the memorial services for Vera Watson and Alison Chadwick upon the expedition's return.

The publicity before the climb had a lot of people wondering, "Can

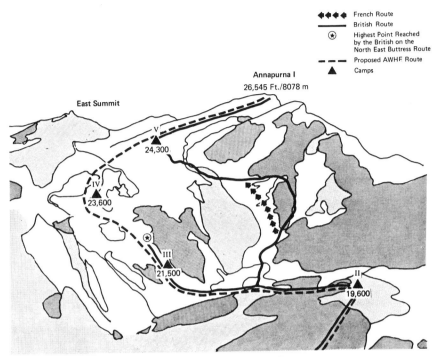

Routes map, Annapurna I

PIRO KRAMAR, expedition physician; ascent of Mount McKinley; ophthalmologist, U.S. Public Health Service Hospital and University of Washington, Seattle, Washington.

IRENE MILLER, treasurer; many ascents in Peru, including new route on Huascarán, Huantsan Norte and new route on Huandoy Sur; a number of technical all-woman ascents, including the north face of Grand Teton; physicist, Palo Alto, California.

MARGI RUSMORE, shipping; ascent of Mount McKinley at age seventeen; earth sciences student, University of California, Santa Cruz.

VERA WATSON, overall coordinator; first woman solo of Aconcagua, highest peak in the Western Hemisphere; all-woman ascents of Mount Robson, Canada, Mount Sajama, Bolivia; first ascents in Alaska; computer programmer, Stanford, California. Deceased.

ANN WHITEHOUSE, packing; ascent of Mount McKinley at age eighteen; student at the College of Nursing, University of Wyoming, Laramie.

women do it?" Whatever the outcome, it was for the world to see. I was exhilarated when they made it to the top, and grieved to hear of the deaths. Now that it's over, I ask Arlene, who organized it all, how she feels.

"Overall, I think the impact of the climb has been very positive in chipping away prejudice and helping more women realize their potential. I don't think the way to change things is to say that either men or women are stronger or have more endurance, but rather to open people up to recognizing that women have the ability to do just about anything, just the way men do.

"But Annapurna is very dangerous. For me, no mountain is worth a life. A year after our climb three more Americans were killed by avalanches. The irony is that Vera and Alison died, not from the avalanches we feared, but from a slip, a misstep, the kind of accident you can have climbing anywhere." Arlene's account of the climb, *A Woman's Place Is on Top, Annapurna*, is due for publication soon.

Several of the women on the climb were forty and over. Some of them are mothers. Arlene says, "When I give my slide show, I mention Christy Tews, our base-camp manager, as a former housewife from Kansas and mother of two. Christy didn't begin to climb until she was thirty-five. When women hear this I notice a rustle of pleasure in the audience. I hope that the more women hear about the success of the climb the more they will be encouraged to try something they really want to do, and it doesn't have to be climbing mountains."

I had heard that there was a conflict over the leadership of the expedition. This is not surprising; expeditions are often filled with tensions arising from the presence of strong personalities. "Yes," Arlene said, "there were difficulties in the beginning between myself and Joan Firey, but we came out of it respecting each other. Leadership, that's one very good reason for all-women activities, to give women the experience of being leaders. Almost invariably in mixed groups men tend to be in the leadership positions, though not always. Women need the experience of leadership in order to gain self-confidence.

"But, China, when you ask me about what's heroic for women, I confess that the word itself reminds me of the military terminology so often used in climbing, such as 'conquering the summit,' making an 'assault' on the mountain. That's ridiculous. You can't 'conquer' a mountain. You climb because the mountain permits it. You are on top for a moment but then all signs of your presence vanish. I climb because I enjoy it, not to prove anything.

"Climbing Annapurna is just one of many accomplishments that help encourage women. It's symbolic, visible. But the mother of four who tackled her own fears by sailing inspired her friend enough to write to you. That helps too. I don't think you can say that one is more laudable than the other."

I talk with Irene Miller, one of the two climbers who made the summit of Annapurna, both before and after the climb. The person I meet upon the return is much stronger, more clear-cut. In addition to being interested in the Annapurna climbers, I had gone to see Irene because she is the mother of two daughters as well as being a successful physicist. She has deliberately chosen to work part time over the years because she's been "as interested in what goes on at home as I am in what goes on at work." This is what appeals to me, her willingness to maintain the value of both work and home in her day-to-day life. So often one is sacrificed for the other.

I remember Irene telling me about her nightmares and fears before the expedition. They continued, she says, and were realized. "The avalanches were worse than any I imagined. There were several times when I would have gladly turned back. One morning there were four avalanches before ten o'clock. Both Arlene and I considered stopping

CLIMBING ACONCAGUA
for Vera Watson

*In the sudden storm
we lost ourselves, the white
darkness settling on us
neither blind nor seeing*

*There was no east, no ascent
only the rope of wind
pulling me in deep, deeper*

*Ahead, the swirls
of their bodies thickened
The four rucksacks turned
to a flurry of blue
vanished and I was left
dumb, my legs instinctive*

—

*When my body wanted
to turn to snow
the storm stopped
I found myself near
a rock wall sheeted with ice
where I saw clearly
a woman's boot
her leg bone in it
clean and frozen*

A black boot, a bone
something so simple
Held as when I was
a child and kept
a violet in an icecube
all summer long
Is this the way

my parka a red jewel
glowing through ice
my backbone printed
in ice
a fern leaf from when
this earth was warm

Is this the way

not my father
tucked in the earth
with the bronze angels
or my friend swallowed
by the tide, her limbs
unraveling into microscopic
threads of green and brown
inseparable from algae

not grandmother
home from the crematorium
in a cardboard box
her fine body
changed to porcelain
less than one of her teacups broken
when we emptied her into a blue
silk scarf and buried
it in the garden, wrapped
so small, a bird
torn by the cat

ice
a wreath of white
who
was she
The field sloped up
to a pale green sky
where I saw three suns
without surprise

then, in a clear place
sheltered by rocks
I pitched this tent

When I woke it was too dark
Someone was near
Even in my sleep I heard

at that point. But the mountain quieted down, and so as a group we decided to go on."

Already in her forties when plans for the climb started, she looked forward to the climb. "You can't wait forever; your body finally gives out. I've wanted to have the experience of being involved with something big with just women. The expedition was it."

"How was it on top?" I ask her.

"It was tremendously exciting. When we got within one hundred yards of the top, one of the sherpas started racing to find the highest point. We found it and took our pictures. We were able to stay up there about twenty minutes. We could see into Tibet, see the reds and browns of the dry desert country broken here and there by a few snow-capped peaks.

"Getting to the summit took one hundred ten percent of what I had. We were fortunate to have good weather, clear, no wind until we got up to the summit. We had to cross a lot of breakable crust, snow that's frozen solid for an inch or so, then deep powder underneath. It's very tiring to move on, and if there had been too much more of it, we could have been stopped. But we all wanted to make the summit. The whole

day I was filled with the thought 'We're going to make it to the top.' There was nothing between us and the summit but our effort.

"We peered over the south face of Annapurna, a route taken by another expedition, which is a breathtaking view of the mountain that drops away several thousand feet at that point.

"It's hard to describe the exhilaration of reaching the summit. It's one of the high points of my life."

"You wouldn't say the high point?" I ask her.

"No, just one of them. Having a baby is a high point much in the same way; you must know about that," Irene says.

Irene, who was the treasurer for AWHE, watched thousands of dollars pour in from people all over the country to support the expedition, from women and men alike. Along with money came letters of encouragement and support. Volunteers sold T-shirts reading "A Woman's Place is on Top" commemorating the climb. The climbers felt a tremendous pressure to succeed. "If we had a falling out, that would be ammunition for people to say, 'See, women can't do anything together,'" said Irene. They did succeed, and yet two died. I ask Irene how she received the report.

"News of the deaths was greeted with sorrow mixed with an incredible sense of survival," Irene said. "It wasn't when but *if* any of us were going to get out. We were angry—it seemed totally unjust—to have lost people by a simple accident, not even the avalanches we feared. We were angry with them for dying. Angry with the mountain for taking them. And that was all mixed with being incredibly relieved to be alive ourselves. I don't think we dealt with it very well. In fact, some people didn't deal with it at all. We only began coming to terms with what happened much later."

People have criticized the climb because of the deaths. People have criticized it because of the male sherpas who accompanied the climbers to the top, saying that it wasn't an all-women's climb, that they were following the traditional path of masculine accomplishments. You will have to draw your own conclusions. I can't criticize them on those accounts. I found the climb both inspiring and encouraging. It was a symbolic event that caught many people's imagination, including my own. While the expedition was under way, in the morning when I would run I would go farther, feeling that they covered a distance for us all.

Last I spoke with Joan Firey, another expedition member, about the climb. Joan has been climbing for thirty years. She married late and had three children, but through it all she has continued to climb, always maintaining an identity of her own. She is a physical therapist by profession, and a painter who signs Joan Wilshire (her maiden name) to her work.

the ring of a piton
splitting into my ear

A moment
of cruel happiness
waiting for the face
to break the dark
Nothing   air
ringing in the ice
shale falling, not footsteps

I am breathing fast
demanding more from the thin air
My body in its down cocoon
is warm, returned
Slowly I have melted snow
stirred in brown cubes of soup
With my face close to the low steam
I sang all the songs I know

Now by flashlight I am writing
like all survivors
I have thought of those
south of here who tossed
their gold watches into the ice
to free themselves of one more burden
who lived on penguin bones
they thawed in their teeth
and of her
outside
suspended in ice

My shadow is thrown large
against the tent
I am that close
to my own life

At this moment I am with no one
in my past   even the wind
is blowing somewhere else
Inside me I feel
something willing
I want to write it here
but it is beginning too far in
to reach this way

I am closer
to the black Andean night, closer
to the stars below me
glittering and distinct:
a ring of animal eyes
looking up from the odd world
—FRANCES MAYES

DEAR AMERICAN WOMEN'S
HIMALAYAN EXPEDITION:

*I assume that some or all of
these women belong to women's
liberation movement. This money
($20) comes to you from an anti-
women's libber who nevertheless
admires their courage and wishes
them luck in the success in the
venture. Please accept. . . . I work
as a press operator in a small factory
and do not have a lot of money, but
if you fall short of your money goal,
just prior to your scheduled
departure, write to me and maybe
I will be able to donate a little more
($50). Any more than that (up to
$2000) would have to be on a trust
as an interest free loan. That's how
much for some reason that expedition
of yours means to me.*
    —letter from a male supporter
                  of AWHE

Members of the Annapurna Expedition, 1978

We talked about the query "Why all-women?" which she often faces.
"It's fun!" she said. "I began climbing with women in 1973, an activity
which has become a great source of joy and friendship." For years Joan
climbed with men. In particular she climbed with her former husband,
until she gradually realized that she was the more aggressive climber
of the two, which created friction. She also points out that any major
Himalayan expedition with a mixed team would have been likely to
leave women in secondary or token positions on a summit team, since
only a small number of climbers on any expedition make the summit.

The expedition wasn't really Joan's kind of climb, but she couldn't
resist the opportunity to take part. For Joan, the excitement of
mountaineering comes from going to a place where no one has ever
been before, a place where she can establish her own route and find a
new way.

The leadership conflict which had existed in the beginning between
her and Arlene became a moot point once the climb got under way.
Joan became ill and had to stop at 21,000 feet. Her illness continued
for the remainder of the expedition, and upon her return to the States

Joan discovered that she was terminally ill. Death again. We speak of Vera's and Alison's death and Joan's struggle to come to terms straightforwardly with her own. "Though I must face the fact of not pulling out of this illness, I have taken the attitude from the beginning that I will."

Joan mentions a theory of death that she heard not long ago, which holds that death is a choice we make. Death an accident? A choice? It is always impending. Joan speaks with the candor of those in the midst of the encounter.

"Confronting death . . . leads to an expansion of the self. A lot of women haven't faced this. Risk taking. I thought that women didn't need to do that so much before we did the climb. Now my opinion might be changed."

Exploring the heroic has led me out of one wilderness into another. Each of the women I mention here embodies some aspect of what might be considered heroic. They are brave, one and all, and all in different ways. There are many more who could be included. What I have written is far from a final chapter on the subject, but serves as a record of a process of rethinking that I've begun.

When I think of this subject I am reminded of Nobel Peace Prize winner Mairead Corrigan's comment "Women have to create new heroes." Dr. Laura Bonaparte is one of mine. I first heard of her through our local Amnesty International office.

Dr. Laura Bonaparte, Argentine psychologist, lives in the wilderness of dictatorship and torture. Since 1975 she has lost five members of her immediate family to the junta. Three of those five have simply been noted by the military as "disappeared." For years she has not known whether they are dead or alive. Laura's daughter Noni was kidnapped while teaching in a *villa de misera*, a shanty town, outside of Buenos Aires during a periodic military sweep. Laura and her husband filed suit against the army. Noni's hands were delivered to her in a glass jar. Officials have now admitted that Noni is dead. Noni's husband was gunned down in the street. Laura's husband, Santiago, was kidnapped and has never been heard from again. Another daughter, Irene, and her husband, Mario, were also kidnapped and have never been heard from again. Irene's two infant children were left in a lobby with their grandparents' address pinned on them.

In a talk at the Pacific School of Religion in Berkeley, Laura said that there are two basic choices: life or death. "To remain silent, to accept the crime, is to acquiesce to the power of death, to give further power to the enemy. To choose life one must speak out, to denounce the enemy." And yet to denounce the enemy may cause further harm to those you love. This is the dilemma of those who remain free. In resolving this for herself, Laura said, "One must realize that it is the

Joan Firey died on February 16, 1980, in Seattle, Washington.

Amnesty International, whose work to release prisoners of conscience around the world won the Nobel Peace Prize in 1977, has documented the existence of more than sixty concentration camps in Argentina. Over twenty thousand people there have been reported "missing" or "disappeared" as of this writing.

enemy who controls the life or death of the loved one, and if speaking out causes death, it is the assassins who have perpetrated this murder, not I."

Laura goes on to relate that when she first lost her daughter and her husband she was isolated by her fears for them. But this began to change as she began to denounce their "disappearance," and as other family members "disappeared" she found more and more people sharing her dilemma. Laura began to speak publicly for all the people who have "disappeared." No longer isolated by her fears for her family, she began to feel a solidarity with all captured peoples, the world over. She has traveled all over the United States and Europe for Amnesty International, contacting people and institutions, speaking and testifying on behalf of herself and thousands of other people who have lost family members to state terrorism. I write to her. We begin to correspond.

Laura Bonaparte's story of contemporary heroism illuminates the whole subject. She takes risks, confronts fear and dangers, but the danger she confronts wears a human face. She has endured great loss and pain and yet, rather than describing herself as bereft, she is enlarged and chooses to consider herself "the mother of all disappeared children." She has reason to hate, and yet she loves. Her anger has galvanized her into action which requires great courage and understanding. She has refused, as a woman, to join in the conspiracy of niceness; this conspiracy, the result of an upbringing that allows no place for anger, hobbles women as effectively as the Chinese practice of foot binding, by teaching that it is unacceptable to engage in conflict. Anger may be the most troublesome and volatile of emotions, but it sharpens the mind. Rather than directing anger at people, acknowledging anger when it arises within and using its heat wisely is the goal. Laura Bonaparte uses her anger as a gift as well as a weapon. Through her anger, she redeems herself from despair and helplessness.

That Laura advocates love, not the hate she might, sounds a depth of compassion and magnanimity that I did not know was possible. Now knowing, I must acknowledge greater possibilities; for whatever one of us can be, we can all become.

Each one of these women has shown me different facets of a new heroic. Each in her own way sets a different course from the traditional notions of conquering and victory. The willingness to follow one's own path, the valuing of sustenance and nurturance, the willingness to speak out on behalf of others, the courage to include one's fears, to face the danger, to take risks, to make the obstacle the path, to stand on the side of life quietly and tenaciously, with compassion, to be fully awake are all part of a heritage that we must claim now. The ideal of the Bodhisattva, "No one is saved until we are all saved," encompasses all notions of saving anything, whether it be an endangered species, the community, or your own soul.

Each one of these women has set out on her own path distinctly. And their paths differ. Perhaps the most important element that they all have in common is the interior act: they have each made a decision to embark. The way is not easy: it is fraught with danger; all the old stories, old and new, tell us so. Do not set out thinking that you can ever return to where you are now. You will be changed, perhaps unrecognizably so. But, if you are successful, you will return home and know it for the first time.

Each life is a heroic quest. It is a journey of the spirit during which we discover our purpose. We have only to embark, to set out in our own hearts, on this journey we began so long ago.

Because the virtues of the mountains are high and wide, the power to ride the clouds is always penetrated from the mountains . . .

—DOGEN,
Mountains and River Sutra

VI   How We Got Back

VI

How We Got Back
natural practices, women and spirituality

*They [the Taoists] went off into forests and
mountains seeking to understand Nature
with the awareness that only through a deep
knowledge of Nature could human beings
hope to live in order.*
——DOLORES LA CHAPELLE,
Earth Wisdom

n fall of 1975 I met Erica Fielder, Randi Dubois, and Kat
Kipping. Our energies were pooled and we formed Women
in the Wilderness in order to meet and support women seeking
outdoor experience. In addition to sharing my love of being
in the wilderness, Erica shared and supported my sense
that somehow, somewhere, we need to include a spiritual dimension
in our lives. We began that New Year of 1976 together at the Audubon
Canyon Ranch in northern California. We spent the weekend fasting,
hiking, and reading to each other from our journals. Anne Styron joined
us. We took an early-morning walk in the hills in the rain. We lay in
the mud, painted our faces with it, streaked down the hillside through
it. Like the Native Americans who had inhabited this place, we sewed
"dream pillows," filling them with mugwort, a local herb believed to
help bring dreams, dreams being voices of the spirits. Subsequently, I
have met more women who share these interests; I discover I am hardly
alone in my search for a spiritual path.

 Erica, unlike me, lives in the middle of the city, but in her garden
she finds ways to connect with nature. In one of the first *Women in the
Wilderness* quarterlies, in 1976, she wrote about celebrating her
connection:

> Just as naturally as the birds fly and
> the ocean waves beat rhythmically against
> the shores, so too did ancient women
> and men tap out their fears, their
> ecstasies on the Earth in music and dance.

*The women's revolution has
everything to do with the search for
ultimate meaning and reality which
some would call God.*

——MARY DALY,
Beyond God the Father

I live in a solid cement and glass city.
Between the cracks grow gardens and parks.
The edges of the cement are swept by wind
and waves. The glass reflects the flight
of birds and clouds.

In this environment I have a choice to make.
I can stand on top of a hill and regret the city's
debris, broken beer bottles, litter, and hear
the whine of heavy traffic below and call this
our "victory" over nature. Or I can stretch
my arms wide, and feel attached to the sun,
the air, wood, water, soil. I can choose
to connect with the natural world and thus
bonded, feel the earth's ancient rhythms even
in the chaos of the city.

As a city dweller I celebrate Earthdays.
I plant by the moon, then drink tea in my
garden. At the Summer Equinox and Winter
Solstice I make small packets of herbal tea
gathered from the woods and parks around San
Francisco. I send these to my friends all
over the world to drink with me at a
particular time on these special days. I have
celebrated the full moon with a walk on
Mt. Tamalpais. . . . I have made masks and thrown
burning embers to the sea to mark the
Winter Solstice.

I begin to discover the old ways, read of ancient spiritual practices, find forms outside my own tradition that make sense to me. Earthdays, equinox, solstice, full moon, these passages of the seasons have always been observed and celebrated by traditional peoples. The rhythms of life, our earthly cycles from which we are now so estranged, I turn to with new eyes. I discover the older traditional feasts behind the Christian holidays. Yet I was raised a Roman Catholic and Christianity is my heritage. Once more I return.

Shortly after our New Year's weekend, I retreat to a tiny Catholic monastery in the wilderness of New Mexico. Walking over moonlit snow to matins at three-fifteen in the morning, mass and communion at six in the morning, the angelus at noon, evening vespers, eating silent meals with the monks—I am thrown back into familiar memories from years of convent school. I have days to wander down into the snow-filled canyon, along the river, to watch a hawk's shadow fly across the field. The silence of the desert snow allows the voice within to be heard. I am both at home and oddly out of place. I find myself spending increasing amounts of time in a side chapel with an unpainted wooden statue of the Blessed Mother. I can almost identify with her, a woman and a mother. Yet her absolute purity and goodness keep her remote. In my meditations, I am drawn to Kali, the devouring mother of the

All true wisdom is only to be learned far from the dwellings of men, out in the great solitudes. . . . To learn to see, to learn to hear, you must do this——go into the wilderness alone. For it is not I who can teach you the ways of the gods. Such things are learned only in solitude.

—IGJUGARJUK, Cribou shaman, in Joan Halifax, *Shamanic Voices*

Hindu pantheon; she is both life-giving and death-dealing, the light and the dark. Mary is only light. She has been divested of the dark and is the poorer for it. I admire her purity, but in contrast, the existence of my body seems enough to damn me. The Church has neatly relieved the Madonna of sexuality by making her brush with human flesh "immaculate," her union divine, the birth virginal. I find that I cannot return.

I am at odds interiorly with my own tradition. So are many other women. I attend a gathering of women on spirituality entitled "Dream of a Common Language" (after the title of Adrienne Rich's collection of poems). We see that traditional religions set up a hierarchy of being, whether implicit or explicit, in which man is at the top; women, native peoples, children, animals, plants, and the Earth itself are under his dominion and afforded status in descending order.

Though scholars still debate the meaning of the biblical passages, the effect of the creation story has been to provide a bulwark for a hierarchical concept of being. This is one of Western society's underlying premises. At the gathering we see that this is not our language. We see that "dominion" has become domination. We see creation destroyed in the name of dominion and what some are now trying to call stewardship. We see that in this hierarchy of being the lower forms are but for man's use. Man's work is to govern these lesser forms, distribute their benefits, and wage war over that which man has dominion. We see that this is not natural. We see that this is against nature. Woman's legendary role in humanity's fall from grace made matters worse. The Judeo-Christian tradition as a whole is embedded in a negative view of women. Genesis and the concept of dominion have been used against us all, women and men alike.

In contrast, in some pre-Christian traditions the Garden was interpreted as a grove of blessedness, the serpent as wise, the mythical tree tended by a priestess willing to impart the gift of knowledge to those who sought it. John Armstrong's book *The Paradise Myth* is one that examines earlier versions of the Garden myth which involved worship of the goddess of fertility. The biblical Garden story is considered by some scholars, such as Joseph Campbell, to be the reverse of the earlier stories which came from the pre-Christian era of goddess worship. Merlin Stone's book *When God Was a Woman* is one of the many works now available on the goddess.

Any thinking about women and spirituality leads one to look again at the phenomenon of witchcraft and the witch hunts of medieval Europe. Witches were most often women who were believed to have great spiritual powers and an intimate knowledge of the natural world, particularly of plants and their uses for healing. Paracelsus, the "father of modern medicine," burned his texts in 1527 and confessed that he

The despising of the feminine soul has been the cause of some of our greatest errors and disasters.
—ROBERT BLY,
Sleepers Joining Hands

Scholars debate the number of people killed during the European witch hunts. Estimates range from 300,000 to 9,000,000.

There are men who in this art exceed the spirits of hell. I have seen the limbs forced asunder, the eyes driven out of the head, the feet torn from the legs, the sinews twisted from the joints, the shoulder blades wrung from their place, the deep veins swollen, the superficial veins driven in, the victim now hoisted aloft and now dropped, now revolved around, head undermost and feet uppermost. I have seen the executioner flog with the scourge, and smite with rods, and crush with screws, and load down with weights, and stick with needles, and bind around with cords, and burn with brimstone, and baste with oil and singe with torches.
—from testimony of a witness, the European witch hunts, in Mary Daly, *Gyn/Ecology*

had learned from the Sorceress all that he knew. The reversal of the Garden story, which gave a negative interpretation to women's role, helped to justify the terrible witch hunts.

The priests and ministers who interpreted God's will as expounded in the biblical stories were led to the cruelest excesses. Over a three-hundred-year period, from the 1400s to the 1700s, churches claimed the lives of several hundred thousand people in the name of Christ. Eighty-five percent of them were women, many of them midwives and healers. These persecutions were the witch hunts. It is difficult to grasp the virulence and hatred that were engendered by the ministers and priests. Reading of them makes me weep. Yet little is made of the witch hunts in the history books. Only now, as women's history is coming to light, can we begin to grasp that the hunts were as horrible and on as large a scale as was Hitler's plot against the Jews. Mary Daly's book *Gyn/Ecology* gives a scathing perspective on the realities of the witch trials and tortures and their historical treatment by male scholarship, to which I am greatly indebted.

Historically, the witch hunts coincided with the professionalization and rise of medicine, and in addition to massacring hundreds of thousands, even millions of women, served to break the continuity of women's culture and knowledge of midwifery and natural healing. Only recently have we begun to take health and healing back into our own hands. Much of what was considered witchcraft were in fact native healing methods, which are being revived today in the name of holistic healing and alternative medicine. Delivery by midwives is becoming increasingly common again.

But in the Middle Ages, if a woman dared to cure without having studied, she was a witch, the fourteenth-century Church declared, and therefore doomed. And, because women were not allowed to study, any female healer was, by definition, a witch. The offenses of healers might be as simple as administering the herbal preparation of ergot, known among midwives to ease labor pains. But, since the Church held labor pains to be the "Lord's just punishment for original sin," it was considered sinful to attempt to relieve them.

Women's sexuality damned them as witches. Written by two Dominican priests in 1484, the official Church document *The Malleus Maleficarum (The Hammer of Witches)* declared that "all witchcraft comes from carnal lust, which is in women insatiable." Men were less susceptible "since Jesus died to preserve the male sex from so great a crime."* The mind turned against the flesh, and in this madness tore apart the body.

Today we are in the death throes of our sexually stereotypic roles.

* Quoted in Mary Daly's *Gyn/Ecology*, p. 200.

It has become far less possible to persecute women on purely sexual grounds, although subtler bases for discrimination persist. To avoid the pitfall of one-dimensional stereotyping, any conception of woman now must encompass and reclaim what the East has always kept: the terrible mother, woman as death dealer as well as life giver, devourer as well as nurturer. The two figures are not separate, they are one being that includes both aspects, as well as many others.

In addition to the biases of history and culture which have omitted much of our past as women, the dualism that runs through much of Western philosophy has tended to leave us with the extreme images of woman as either virgin or witch. Only now are the options between these absolutes becoming evident.

The grand mistake of Western philosophy, its terminal disease, was the division of spirit and flesh. The Platonic ideal located reality elsewhere, the temporal realm was but an imitation or copy of an ideal. Judeo-Christian theology went on to reject the body as sinful, an instrument of the devil. Man was associated with mind and spirit, the higher form of being, and woman with the flesh. But, contrary to the dogmas of organized Western religions, the mystical traditions of both East and West meet in the affirmation that the body, the earth, the flesh, the material world, are one with the world of the spirit. This union is the mystery. Life is the dream awake.

No more Church, Catholicism only furthers the distortion. I strike out on my own, taking clues from the pre-Christian era. I consider myself a pagan for the time, a person of the countryside, which is what *paganos*, the original Greek word, meant. It will have to do.

THE PHILOSOPHER'S JOURNEY

"If this is so," the other commented, "philosophy has up to the present been on the wrong track."

"That is so," said Pan. "Philosophy is an immoral practice because it suggests a standard of practice impossible of being followed, and which, if it could be followed, would lead to the great sin of sterility."

"The idea of virtue," said the Philosopher, with some indignation, "has animated the noblest intellects of the world."

"It has not animated them," replied Pan, "it has hypnotised them so that they have conceived virtue as repression and self-sacrifice as an honourable thing instead of the suicide which it is."

"Indeed," said the Philosopher, "this is very interesting, and if it is true the whole conduct of life will have to be very much simplified."

"Life is already simple," said Pan, "it is to be born and to die, and in the interval to eat and drink, to dance and sing, to marry and beget children."

"But it is simply materialism," cried the Philosopher.

"Why do you say 'but'?" replied Pan.

"It is sheer, unredeemed animalism," continued his visitor.

"It is any name you please to call it," replied Pan.

"You have proved nothing," the Philosopher shouted.

"What can be sensed requires no proof."

—JAMES STEPHENS,
The Crock of Gold

SPRING 1978

Denise Partida, a close friend of mine from Texas, calls to tell me that she is at the hospital with her six-year-old son, Adan, who is dying. He is Benjamin's best friend. It is five in the morning. Adan has had serious heart problems since the day he was born, but we all thought he was doing well after massive surgeries and rerouting of his arteries. Then yesterday he simply passed out while playing in his room with his sisters. Denise knows that this time there is no hope. She calls me to tell me that she is going to have him cremated and that she wants to send me his ashes to scatter at sea. She refuses to bury him in the ground. She wants him to rest with the sea creatures, especially the whales, that have captured his love and imagination. "Can't you come yourself?" I ask. "No, it's impossible, you must do it for me."

I am stunned at her request and yet I know I must say yes. She will call back soon; she must go back to him, in intensive care. I go to the kitchen to fix a cup of coffee, but never drink it. I will keep a vigil with my friend Adan. And as I sit I feel his passing: passing, not dying. I know he is dying and yet I have a strong sense of his entering into a larger continuum; he is dying, but it is not what I have thought it to be before. The phone rings. I am told that he is dead. I grasp for the first time that "death" is our way of talking about this mysterious event that we can never understand until we make it our own. How can I convey this to my children, his friends?

Sadly, I leave the house and go out walking up the hillside to the sea cliffs, and sit for hours looking at the Pacific, watching the waves crash and swirl over the rocks far below. Observe. I want to mark his passage. This will not be a funeral, I decide. Suddenly it comes to me. I recall having read not long ago about a man, Jim Nollman, who plays music with whales. I resolve to contact him.

A few days later I find him in Bolinas.

Yes, he says, he will help, and instructs me to find a sailboat to take to sea. Soon the whales will be passing off the coast on their migration to Baja, and there is a good chance that we will see them. Jim will be lowered into the water in his wet suit with his whale drum and he will play to communicate the occasion of our meeting to them. Communicating with whales sounds crazy to me, but who knows? My intuition says go ahead.

The next day I hitchhike into town to pick up my car which is being repaired. Tom, who gives me a ride, is a shipwright who has sailed his own boat to Hawaii and back. "How big is it?" I inquire. "Thirty-six feet." "I've just been asked to scatter the ashes of one of my children's

Jim Nollman, Tom, and the whale drum

friends at sea. I'm looking for a boat. Would you help by sailing us to the Farallones?"

"Yes," he says, no hesitation. We exchange phone numbers. I will call him in a few days. The passage is beginning to take shape. I call Denise and she tells me that a friend has given her a plane ticket to come to San Francisco. I am relieved that she will come and scatter the ashes herself. She approves the plan. She will arrive in two weeks.

Finally the evening before we are to set out to sea comes. Denise has arrived. A handful of friends and relatives gather at my home. Jim Nollman joins us. I light a large fire in the fireplace and we begin to talk about tomorrow. Our friend Will Janus shows us his film about whales. Jim begins to play the vihuela, a Portuguese string instrument, as I read from my journal of the morning that Adan died:

> Do not hesitate: do not be afraid. Life depends on this moment. This is the way in deeper. Mark it well, affirm it, celebrate and give thanks for being able to take part, to share in this moment when the veil that shrouds the mystery has been pulled back. Know that in the world over, many are dying and being born at this moment, just as these waves below ebb and flow over the rocks. That this time and these preparations are not only for Adan. He is the opening, the opportunity to affirm and be more fully alive. For life feeds on death. His death does not diminish me. I am broken, broken open, enlarged, able to let more pass through me. I am humbled and grateful. May the most fitting way for us to honor his passing come.

We sit quietly by the fire. The mothers, Denise and I, hold one another. Jan Lovett Keen picks up her flute and begins to play with Jim; friends gather round Denise. The dogs howl. Midnight.

We waken at three-forty-five in the morning. It is the vernal equinox, the first day of spring. We eat quickly and leave for Sausalito, where the boat is docked. By six in the morning we are under way. The harbor bell is ringing. Dawn. The day is clear and windy.

The children fall asleep below as we sail under the Golden Gate Bridge. By eight-thirty in the morning we have seen two California gray whales. Tom sets a course to take us directly into their path. We sail on for another two hours or so. Denise sits thoughtfully, holding the box of ashes in her lap. The water sparkles in the midmorning sun, the brightness blinding. Suddenly the surface near us foams and breaks, a whale breaches in a shimmering leap; we all laugh in delight at being so close to this creature. It's as though we are being greeted. We are in the whale's path at last.

We see two gray whales playing closer. For over an hour we sail toward the Farallon Islands and they swim nearby, rolling, splashing. We tack and move within a hundred feet of the whales. We lower Jim overboard in his wet suit, the drum rigged to float in a frame with him. The rubber mallet he draws across the drum's surface makes sounds much like those of the whales themselves. They continue to roll and play nearby. We all stand quietly watching Jim floating on the water, connected to us by a yellow lifeline, and the whales, crusty with barnacles, blow. Soon he is chilled and signals us to pull him in. Once he's back in the boat, I realize that it is time to scatter the ashes and that Denise is not going to be the one to say so. I will have to tell her. She agrees that we should scatter the ashes while the whales are still with us. It has been remarkable enough that these two whales have stayed nearby over an hour: they might sound at any moment and be gone.

Tom drops the mainsail and we gather on the foredeck, reaching out in a circle of hands for children, friends, and strangers no longer strangers. "Spirit, guide us on our own paths as the whales are guided, instinctively, with grace. Bless this passage of Adan's which we call death."

Denise begins to pry open the box in which the ashes are sealed. Her long hair blows in the wind like waves of dark water. When the box is open, she leans over the side, scattering the ashes to the wind and water. The ashes are not uniform and fine as from a hearth; they are bony clumps of what has been a child's body, now chalk-white, blowing over the waves, falling for an instant on the surface, light, then dark, then gone, we are done, he is released, free.

Rites of passage, celebrations of the changing seasons, now obscured from us for the most part, provide a way for us to mark important transitions, both personal and seasonal. More and more women are returning to observations of the solstice, equinox, the full moon, and are creating rites of passage for all stages of life. I am concerned about the onset of menstruation.

With two teenage children, I know how critical the passage into puberty is. For the last three summers I have taken Matt and Madelon on a river trip with ten of their friends. I observe their curiosity and the changes made by puberty. I seek to provide an outlet for their energy. I cannot do enough.

Summer of 1979. We take a two-day paddle-raft trip on the American River. We paint our faces on solstice morning, black and white, red and purple, stars around the eyes, moons and flames streaking across foreheads, chins, and cheeks. Amidst whoops and hollers Matt and Madelon dart off with their friends in threes and fours around the campground to wish others Happy Summer Solstice and, in general, shock the population with their unexpected appearance.

This year, 1980, they want more. We plan to go backpacking in the mountains as well as rafting. Could this trip become a rite of passage? Can a mother initiate her son? No, this is where a father must come in. There are very real limits at this juncture of adolescence. I do not know what it means to be a man, but I have some understanding of what it is to be a woman. I can still recall the beginning of menstruation. There will be something I can do for my daughter.

I long to welcome Madelon into womanhood, to celebrate her coming of age. I recall how my mother told me it was "the curse." Her mother told her nothing, so she locked herself in the bathroom for hours in fright at onset of her menses. No one is to blame. This is what happens when we have no rites of passage.

A group from Women in the Wilderness go to the Miwok Village site at Point Reyes National Seashore to dig a menstrual hut just as Miwok Indian women did. The event holds my imagination. It is clear that the Indians treated menstruation differently. I turn to Carolyn Niethammer's book, *Daughters of the Earth, the Lives and Legends of American Indian Women,* to learn about the customs of the traditional people.

Many taboos were associated with the menstruating girl or woman, in Native American tribes as well as other cultures. In some cultures she is believed to have magical powers. In others she is reviled as unclean. Some taboos were designed to protect the tribe from the girl's power, and others, more positive, were designed to protect the girl and ensure her health, strength, and beauty throughout her life. A girl's dreams

during this time were sometimes believed to reveal the guiding spirits that would show her the direction of her life. In some instances, girls as well as boys were sent out into the wilderness on a vision quest at puberty. Among the Papago, there was great celebration, with days of feasting and dancing in honor of the maiden following the initial puberty rite. During the Apache ceremony, the young woman receives the power of Changing Woman, a legendary founder of Apache culture. Often months of preparation go into the four-day ceremony of the Apaches. For the first four days following the main rites, the Apache girl's new power is believed "to be able to cure the sick and to bring rain."

In contrast, the menstruating Ojibwa maiden was taught that she was surrounded by evil spirits. She was regarded as a menace to herself and all living creatures, Niethammer's book tells us. "Dressed in very old clothes, she had to sit in a tiny hut in the forest, soot smeared around her eyes, obsessed and saddened with the terror of herself."

In ancient Celtic tales, the hag's blood is a female symbol of deepest wisdom and a knowledge of opposites.
—SHUTTLE and REDGROVE,
The Wise Wound

Unfortunately, this seems to be analogous to the way many of us felt when we began to menstruate. Many of us still have a negative attitude toward the monthly cycle. It took years for me to accept the fact that the menses would occur each month. Severe cramping accompanied the lack of acceptance until I began to accept my body's rhythm, welcome the recurrent cycle; for me the pain then disappeared.

One can be in harmony with one's cycle, with a positive attitude toward menstruation. *The Wise Wound,* by Penelope Shuttle and Peter Redgrove, is a study of the values of menstruation. It points out that, rather than understanding menstruation, we usually look upon it as a burden. Consequently, millions of women consult doctors for remedies for premenstrual tension, and many receive prescriptions for tranquilizers and other drugs. We are not only insulated from the rhythms of nature, we insulate ourselves from the rhythms of our own bodies by using medicine against ourselves.

Rites of initiation are means of delineating and assimilating the enormous emotional and physical changes we undergo at various points of life, such as puberty. Other cultures tell me that there have been, and continue to be, ways to convey the feelings about the coming of the menses as an event to be celebrated and shared, a cause for joy rather than a source of sorrow and embarrassment.

I am increasingly aware of some secret knowledge that I transmit to my own daughter, Madelon, never in words, about what it is to be a woman. Curious to know more mothers and daughters, and to explore this relationship, I organize a mother-daughter trip on the Stanislaus River in California shortly before her twelfth birthday. Sandi Mardigian, one of the board members of Women in the Wilderness, and her daughter Wendy come. A few years older than I, Sandi has done a lot outdoors with her two daughters, including climbing Mount Kilimanjaro.

The water is extremely high, near flood stage, from the melting mountain snows. Some outfitters have canceled their trips for the weekend. Four women fall out of our boats going through the first and most difficult rapids. Two of them swim to shore, and two we pick up in the boats. A mother and a daughter were separated in the spill. Each thought the other drowned, and their safe reunion on shore minutes later revealed to them the extent of their caring.

Late in the afternoon after we make camp, I ask the group to draw life maps. "The piece of paper represents your life. Make it as long or as short as you want it to be," I explain. I offer crayons, instructing them to pick colors that feel expressive of their life. "Now imagine that your life is like the river we're on. Where does the river of your life begin, where are there bends in the shoreline, where is the rapid that threw you out of the boat, where are the languid stretches of flat

Mother-Daughter Trip, Stanislaus River, Calif.

water, what is the countryside like along your river, where are the eddies that catch you, where is the main current, good campsites, fellow travelers? Draw you life like the river, from beginning to end.

"Let your hand be your guide, and without thinking let the line of your life emerge as a river. Then look over your life, and either by drawing symbols or writing brief narratives, note what specific event is signified by that bend in the river, the rapids, the flat water, the impassable waterfall where you had to get off the river and portage." We each drift off on our own.

An hour later I look and find mothers and daughters huddled together on the grass, eagerly sharing their maps with each other. Each map is unique but when clustered together the maps reveal patterns of change that we all undergo, and pool around certain stages of life, such as puberty.

My daughter, Madelon, and I share our own maps. I am struck by the way she perceived events in my life and drew them in her map. A childhood episode I can barely remember she recalls as major, and draws it in detail. She appears in mine as a steady stream of bright blue color that begins when I am twenty-one and weaves its way through until the end.

I recall a comment on the famous myth of mother and daughter, Demeter and Persephone, that rings true: "Demeter searched for her vanished daughter as though she were the lost half of herself." Such intimacy is the beauty and danger of the relationship, and soon Madelon must be on her own.

The weekend trip on the Stanislaus proves to be too crowded and too short to allow an appropriate time to talk much about being mothers and daughters. But it is obvious that each of us has uncovered a deeper level of this tie. It has been a very special time.

I continue to investigate this vein of women's myths, rites of passage, celebrations, pre-Christian practices.

. . . the patriarchal and Protestant heritage of northern Europe . . . is spiritually an empty ruin.

—ROBERT BLY,
Sleepers Joining Hands

Merlin Stone speaks at a conference on "The Re-Emerging Goddess," describing the theories expounded in her book *When God Was a Woman.* After spending ten years traveling and researching the archaeological evidence for her theories, she can review the loss of culture that women experienced when history began to be dated from the birth of the male deity, Christ, and the preceding eight thousand years of worship of the Great Mother were virtually wiped from the record. But the worship of the goddess was not suppressed easily, as the savage and continuing persecution of witches shows. Many interpret witchcraft as a holdover of this earlier religion. Stone points out that if we include the older pre-Christian religions that dominated the ancient world, instead of marking time with Christ's birth, the year is actually 9980. Despite her awareness of this collective loss, Stone is imbued with a sense of excitement and discovery. She is like some early explorer who, after laboring over a difficult and high mountain pass in a storm, has reached a peak from which a whole new world of rivers, valleys, forests, and far mountain ranges is suddenly visible below. Another way of looking at the world unfolds.

Not long after we began to publish the quarterly *Women in the Wilderness,* Erica came across an obscure reference to a seventeenth-century group of monks in Pennsylvania called "The Order of the Woman in the Wilderness." Three years later I began to do the necessary research to find out who these men were.

German Pietists in Europe and followers of the great Christian mystic, Jakob Boehme, the members of the order fled the religious persecution that was raging in Europe. This small band of celibate men came to settle in North America in 1694. Though they had no official name of their own, they were called The Order of the Woman in the Wilderness by their neighbors. They believed devoutly that the end of the world was drawing near and would be marked by the re-emergence of the woman in the Book of the Apocalypse who fled into the wilderness to escape the dragon (Revelation 12:1–17). They held that they must go out into the wilderness or the desert "to perfect themselves in holiness," wrote Julius Sachse in his history of the German Pietists, to pray and make ready for her coming. Her appearance would signal the Second Coming of Christ, also thought to be the end of the world.

The order settled in an area outside of Philadelphia called the Wissahickon Woods. They were alchemists, herbalists, and astronomers, and had a celestial observatory. They were extremely well liked by the township, and gave free education to orphaned children. They planted a large garden, where they raised herbs and plants for healing, "probably the first systematic effort made to raise European medicinal plants for curative purposes in America," according to Sachse. They are described as welcoming all to their devotional services, and honoring divergent opinions. Despite their strong convictions about the impending Apocalypse, they seemed extremely tolerant.

Legend has it that on the seventh anniversary of the community's establishment in the Wissahickon Woods, St. John's Eve (summer solstice), preparations were being made for the ritual lighting of fires on the hillside at nightfall. Suddenly the apparition of a woman emerged out of the woods and appeared to the brothers. "It receded into the shadows of the forest, and appeared again immediately before them as the fairest of the lovely." There was great excitement. Surely this must be the sign they had waited for. The brothers prayed continuously for the next two days and nights. On the third evening, the apparition of the woman appeared again, "but their prayers, instead of availing, always repelled the fair deliverer. After this the apparition did not reappear."

Ten years after the settlement's founding, much had changed. Though new members had come from Europe, others had left the community. Philadelphia had grown and encroached upon the seclusion of the woods, while settlers, formerly only a few hundred Quakers, now numbered in the thousands, and belonged to several different denominations. Still, Kelpius and his followers were held in great esteem, though it was becoming clearer that the community lacked permanence.

Kelpius and a few others continued their spiritual practices but the majority of them felt drawn by the colonies' demand for men of their

THE REVELATION OF
ST. JOHN THE DIVINE
Chapter 12

And there appeared a great wonder in heaven; a woman clothed with the sun, and the moon under her feet, and upon her head a crown of twelve stars:
2. And she being with child cried, travailing in birth, and pained to be delivered.
3. And there appeared another wonder in heaven; and behold a great red dragon, having seven heads and ten horns, and seven crowns upon his heads.
4. And his tail drew the third part of the stars of heaven, and did cast them to the earth: and the dragon stood before the woman which was ready to be delivered, for to devour her child as soon as it was born.
5. And she brought forth a man child who was to rule all nations with a rod of iron: and her child was caught up unto God, and to his throne.
6. And the woman fled into the wilderness, where she hath a place prepared of God, that they should feed her there a thousand two hundred and threescore days.
7. And there was war in heaven: Michael and his angels fought against the dragon: and the dragon fought and his angels,
8. And prevailed not; neither was their place found any more in heaven.
9. And the great dragon was cast out, that old serpent, called the Devil, and Satan, which deceiveth the whole world: he was cast out into the earth, and his angels were cast out with him.
10. And I heard a loud voice saying in heaven, Now is come salvation, and strength, and the kingdom of our God, and the power of his Christ: for the accuser of our brethren is cast down, which accused them before our God day and night.

11. And they overcame him by the blood of the Lamb, and by the word of their testimony; and they loved not their lives unto the death.

12. Therefore rejoice, ye heavens, and ye that dwell in them. Woe to the inhabiters of the earth and of the sea! for the devil is come down unto you, having great wrath, because he knoweth that he hath but a short time.

13. And when the dragon saw that he was cast unto the earth, he persecuted the woman which brought forth the man child.

14. And to the woman were given two wings of a great eagle, that she might fly into the wilderness, into her place, where she is nourished for a time, and times, and half a time, from the face of the serpent.

15. And the serpent cast out of his mouth water as a flood after the woman, that he might cause her to be carried away of the flood.

16. And the earth helped the woman, and the earth opened her mouth, and swallowed up the flood which the dragon cast out of his mouth.

17. And the dragon was wroth with the woman, and went to make war with the remnant of her seed, which keep the commandments of God, and have the testimony of Jesus Christ.

capabilities. Nightly vigils were abandoned, devotional exercises fewer. The great catastrophe they had expected had not occurred. After years of work and prayer, Kelpius died, and though a few ascetics stayed on in the woods, the community disbanded.

In a way I have come to believe what these hermits believed long ago. Psychologically, at least, I count their vision as correct: when the female or nurturing side of existence re-emerges from the wilderness and becomes active within us all, the implicit order of the world will be affirmed. By that I mean, when the values of caring and community replace the values of the marketplace, the world we now know will end, and a new era could then begin. Will it ever occur? We can only live as though it will.

Women in the wilderness, past and present, becomes a recurrent theme. Joseph Campbell gives a lecture entitled "The Woman's Journey." He supplements his talk with slides of a series of paintings done by two of C. G. Jung's patients during a course of treatment. The dilemma of finding the path of womanhood is depicted in paintings of a huge tree bursting through the center of jagged mountains. The woman is also shown as a tree bending over, her arms and hands now roots seeking the earth. Another painting shows her as putting aside the symbols of her Judeo-Christian tradition and diving into her own subconscious. The tradition she inherited is useless to her also. The paintings depict with vivid accuracy the interior crisis facing contemporary women. No myths, no psychic maps of the past will do; we are on our own. The myths will have to come from our own poets and storytellers.

New Year, 1978. Again I make a retreat, this time to a Zen Buddhist monastery. Drawn by the simplicity and nontheistic approach of Zen, I eventually become a practicing student. The center of the Judeo-Christian tradition no longer holds and so I sit zazen in front of a blank wall, meditating, counting my breath—facing the problem of achieving a quiet heart. Through this practice, I formally begin again, grounding myself in an ancient spiritual tradition, within a community.

As I continue to sit, my instincts take me back, saying, Go back to the land. Practice must be connected to place. It is the Native Americans who developed a spiritual practice from this land, their mountains, their rivers. In a belief akin to Taoism they hold that the natural world is sacred and that we are inseparable from all that grows around us. This thinking is implicit in Buddhism and is the root of good ecological practice and natural philosophy.

I laugh to myself as I drive over to talk with Lonna Knight, a Lakota Indian woman, recalling my parents' threat to give me "back to the Indians" when I was a child. Now I seek them out. Christianity is a religion of the city, having long ago severed connection with the land. Seeking a spiritual practice that is compatible with my experience leads me to our native people. They have no "church," no "religion" as such, but they have a way of life, a world view, from which we have much to learn.

My friend Karen Otsea comes with me to see Lonna, who is a member of Women of All Red Nations. She and women from other tribes have organized this group to address women's issues. She tells us the story of White Buffalo Woman, who gave the teachings and the sacred pipe to the Sioux. Lonna lives in a communal house of the American Indian Movement. She invites us to stay for the weekly sweat with the other women in the community. We agree and continue to listen to her stories of White Buffalo Woman until the men have finished their sweat and it is our turn.

We undress and wrap ourselves in large towels and go out into the cold fall night. The firepit is blazing full of rocks heating for the sweat in the Oakland backyard. Just behind the firepit is the sweat lodge. Tana, who is in charge of the ceremony, begins to prepare the pipe as we stand in a circle around the fire. A fire keeper brings a burning braid of sweetgrass and encircles us in its smoke. Finally, Tana is ready and leads the way inside. We enter and move clockwise around another pit of rocks, which are still hot from the men's sweat.

Suddenly I remember that in sweats on wilderness trips in the past I have become claustrophobic and have been unable to stay inside without panicking. I ask Tana if I can sit by the flap. She says no. She sits on one side, her helper on the other. We crawl in, five women, a child, and a four-month-old baby girl; I go into the middle next to Karen. As we enter we say, *"Metakwease,"* which means "all my relations." Soon the flap is closed. My heart sinks in the darkness. Tana begins to speak, explaining that we enter the sweat to be purified. The lodge is the womb of the mother. Here we will pray and share the pipe.

The ceremony begins. Inside the lodge I am inside the cave again. I am inside the womb: the world has disappeared; we are deep inside the earth; we are inside the mother and I am breathless. My heart pounds the moment I say *"Metakwease,* all my relations." In the center is a pit, full of rocks, hot; some are glowing, some have cooled. But the glowing is dull, giving off no light, revealing only the shapes of the rocks themselves. *Metakwease.*

Tana tells us, "We are inside the womb of our mother. When we leave this womb we will be as we were when we left our mothers' wombs, newborn. We enter this lodge to purify ourselves, to pray for our people, to offer the pipe. Hey, Tekansile! Grandfather, Mother,

. . . there are mountains hidden in treasurers; there are mountains hidden in marshes, mountains hidden in the sky; there are mountains hidden in mountains. There is a study of mountains hidden in hiddenness . . .

When we thoroughly study the mountains, this is the mountain training. Such mountains and rivers themselves spontaneously become wise men and sages.

—DOGEN,
Mountains and River Sutra

For the shaman, as for the Tibetan anchorite and most seers and visionaries, nature's wilderness is the locus for the elicitation of the individual's inner wilderness, the great plain of the spirit.

—JOAN HALIFAX,
Shamanic Voices, A Survey of Visionary Narratives

we greet you, we give thanks for this life. *Metakwease,*" she says, pouring the first bowlful of water over the rocks, which hiss and steam. We listen to the song of the rocks, *"Metakwease."* She pours another bowlful of water over the rocks, which hiss, sputter, and pop. We listen. The pounding in my heart slows down as I remember my breathing. If I feel I cannot breathe, Tana tells me, I am to put my face down to Mother Earth; she is cool; I will find the air I need, air chill like the night only an inch away on the other side.

But no, the night is inside and all my demons have come to meet me. My desire to bolt and run is intense; I want out. Panic looms up in my mind, but so does the memory of moments when I have gone into my fears rather than run. "Breathe, stay with your breath," I remind myself. Listen to the prayers of the original people, listen to these people, and to these women who pray for the Earth, who pray for us all; join them, not the panic.

Finally I am calm. Lonna scatters cedar on the glowing rocks. Tana taps each rock with the mouthpiece of the pipe. Tap, tap, tap, tap in the dark. "Five more rocks; these have grown cold." *"Metakwease."* The flap opens, more are brought to us, handed in on a shovel, and added to the pit, where Tana rolls them into place with a deer antler. The cool night air mixing with the hot, steamy atmosphere inside provides a small reprieve. We go on. *"Metakwease,"* all my relations. The flap closes. Again the cedar and the tapping with the pipe. The prayers continue. I listen to the thanks, the greetings, but I hear the sorrow of a people that are dying. Their culture has been broken, but not their spirit. I listen to the sound of that spirit inside this sweat, I feel the spirit swell with the voices, it is catching, I am caught, a woman begins to cry. I cannot breathe and put my face to the dirt for air; its coolness is sweet.

I sit upright again, dripping, soaked in sweat. *"Metakwease,"* my entire body is throbbing, I grow dizzy in the heat. Next we pray. One by one. Now it is my turn; the words spill out without my speaking them: "I am a woman in the wilderness. I come from a people who have lost their way. Help us, Tekansile, Mother Earth, find our way. . . ." Tana calls for the pipe, and begins its clockwise passage around the circle. Each one of us takes the pipe and smokes the strong tobacco. The tobacco makes me even more dizzy, and once the pipe has completed the circle I call out, "All my relations," as my signal that I want to go out. Tana opens the flap and I crawl into the night, revived by the cold air in a moment. Though I am sorry to have left before the end of the ceremony, I have stayed in the sweat for over an hour. I realize that there is no need for apology. I am not as strong as these women, and must be content to be as I am. I know this inside myself. I've sat

The increasing strength of poetry, defense of earth, and mother consciousness, implies that after hundreds of years of being motionless, the Great Mother is moving again in the psyche. Every day her face becomes clearer. We are becoming more sensitive, more open to her influence. She is returning, or we are returning to her; everyone who looks down into his own psyche sees her, just as in leaves floating on a pond you can sometimes make out faces. The pendulum is just now turning away from the high point of father consciousness and starting to sweep down. The pendulum rushes down, the Mothers rush toward us, we can all feel the motion downward, the speed increasing.

—ROBERT BLY,
Sleepers Joining Hands

with my most primitive fears longer in this backyard than in any wilderness, where I could move around, distract myself.

For a change, this is enough. Within five minutes, after shouts and chants, Karen, Lonna, Tana, and the rest of the women pour laughing into the night.

VII   What Currents to Expect
and from Where

VII

What Currents to Expect
and from Where

beyond the movement, the personal is the political

xperiences and thoughts spiral. The Native American movement makes no distinction between the realm of the personal and the realm of the political, nor does Buddhism, nor does feminism, nor does my common sense. The common affirmation is that we are not separate from our environment or from each other. We may be different but we are not separate; and therein lies a perception of another order of women and men, people and environment, feelings and thought.

Native Americans have a way of speaking that expresses a familiar sense of belonging to creation that is as accurate as it is poetic. They say Earth is our Mother, who feeds us and gives us life. She is to be honored, protected, and celebrated. The traditional people would not be surprised at scientists Lynn Margulis and J. E. Lovelock's Gaia hypothesis. It proposes that the Earth is alive: "the biosphere is a self-regulating entity with the capacity to keep our planet healthy by controlling the chemical and physical environment." Outside the mainstream of science, Margulis and Lovelock's theory seems to be a reiteration of the Native American's view. Lovelock writes of Earth as though she were an organism herself. Their theory is named Gaia in honor of the Greek goddess Gaia, the Mother Earth.

Earth as female, Nature as a woman has been linked historically throughout all cultures. Erich Neumann's study *The Great Mother* contains numerous photos of ancient artifacts from all over the world depicting woman as Nature in her various forms: the Great Mother, the Goddess of Fertility, the Goddess of the Tree of Life, the Snake Goddess, the Lady of the Plants, the Lady of the Beasts, Goddess of the Moon, Lady of the Harvest, and Goddess of the Grain. She is Mother Earth and she is also Kali, the devourer and life giver. Other illustrations show her as the Goddess of Death and the Gorgon.

Neumann sees the feminine element of life as the vessel of transformation, which culminates in cultures East and West depicting the figure of wisdom as female. For the Greeks it was Sophia. For Buddhists Prajna-paramita is the perfection of wisdom, the Mother of the Buddhas. Especially revered in Tibetan Buddhism is Tara, the one who leads souls to Nirvana. The Tara Buddha is the highest symbol of spiritual transformation of woman. Again and again, these figures represent an ancient symbolic link between women and the world of nature.

The link between woman and nature is becoming more explicit politically. As I write, final plans are being formulated for a Women and Ecology Conference in the Northeast. Talk has begun of a similar conference here on the West Coast. With other women writers and poets, I am asked to speak at a conference on "Woman and Nature." Women and Ecology, Women in the Wilderness, there is a voice emerging, from the East Coast to the West Coast.

The rationale for the northeastern project, called "Woman and Life on Earth," reads:

> Because we have traditionally been mother, nurse and guardian of the home and community, women have been quick to perceive the threat to the health and lives of our families and neighbors that is posed by nuclear power proliferation, polluted waters and toxic chemicals. As the ecological crisis grows, more and more women are entering into the political sphere to assume leadership in the various ecological movements.

The conference is designed to heighten women's awareness of the environmental crisis, and of the roles we play in it, and to discuss what can be done to alleviate the dangerous situation we have all allowed to develop.

My own awareness was heightened by a brush with cancer. Just before leaving for the ocean-kayaking expedition in Baja, I had the requisite physical and was told to come back for another exam upon my return. I left for Mexico not particularly concerned, but on my return found that cervical and breast cancer might be a possible diagnosis. I had never considered the possibility of serious illness in my life. Now I do. I read the pathologist's report in a state of disbelief. I grow tense, my back knots. Weeks go by, more tests are done. I don't believe what they are telling me. I'm in good health, I run, I meditate, I do all "the right things," and it doesn't matter. I realize that the extent to which we are poisoning our environment leaves us all increasingly vulnerable.

But I am fortunate. The breast lump is removed surgically and found to be benign. The deterioration of the cervix reverses itself and the cervix goes back to normal. The weeks of acupuncture and other commonsense remedies, such as diet and what some might call prayer, take effect.

Women of child-bearing age at the American Cyanamide plant in West Virginia worked with chemicals that posed special risk to fetuses. Women employees protested. Rather than make the plant safe for all workers they were told to be sterilized or lose their jobs.

Alone, without family and friends, I could easily have been lost in the despair that surfaced. I reached out for friends and they were there. The connections themselves were central to the healing. We are vulnerable creatures to whom family and tribe are essential for well-being. Relationships nourish and deepen our ability to care. Yet society tears at this fabric. Technology fosters the illusion that we are self-sufficient, separate, and in control.

The events of private life shape the public forum. The possibility of cancer increased my environmental awareness tenfold. I had thought the statement "the personal is the political" was simplistic; now I understood. The thousands of untested, possibly carcinogenic chemicals we have in our environment begin to register in another way. Thinking I had cancer had initially made me feel helpless. But now I was angry at our senselessness.

At a Women in the Wilderness meeting shortly after the Three Mile Island accident, I found myself pushing for a program on nuclear plants. Our educational programs had been admirably noncontroversial, but in light of the near meltdown in Pennsylvania, lectures on native plant life were hardly enough. We had to be concerned with the world of technology as well as with nature. Other women agreed. Feeling frustrated and helpless about the accident at Three Mile Island was an inadequate response. I had to do something. Not knowing where to begin, I volunteered to organize and chair a panel discussion of women with experience in antinuclear activism. There I would find out.

The evening of our panel comes and at six o'clock sharp at Fort Mason, in San Francisco, the participants appear. We introduce ourselves, sit down to talk, and find ourselves falling into agreement, though we have never met. The commonality of our concerns and approaches is striking. Shortly thereafter we begin the program with a film excerpt of *Dark Circle*, a documentary being made about women in the antinuclear movement by Judy Irving.

I ask each panelist to talk about her life: "How did you arrive at your current position on nuclear power and alternative energy sources?" Liz Walker, from the American Friends Service Committee and Abalone Alliance, begins:

"I was working on the Simple Living project, looking at resource use and the kind of involvement that each of us had in the resources that we were using. We gradually split off, and the area my colleague David Hartsough and I chose was energy. Shortly thereafter we saw *Weil*, a film clip of an antinuclear demonstration in West Germany where twenty-eight thousand people had gone onto the site of a proposed nuclear power plant in the small town of Weil. There were thousands of policemen, but the people just took the power into their own hands and actually built a village on the site of this proposed plant.

Clearly, there are those among us, at least in the women's movement, who recognize the ecological emergency of our time for the profound spiritual failure that it is. They know we are not going to save ourselves with a quick technological fix and more efficient resource management. Rather, the Goddess is going to have to be reborn in our midst, not simply as a systems analyst's hypothesis, but as living culture. Where the movement for women's liberation reaches to that awareness, it becomes something far larger and stronger than another political cause.

—THEODORE ROSZAK,
Person/Planet

"We were inspired. So Dave and I looked around and saw a similar type of organization building up in the Clamshell Alliance on the East Coast, and we thought, Why not in California? We talked with other people around the state and many felt that it was time; they were disillusioned by the current power structure and the idea of nuclear-generated electricity and all the hazards involved. We decided to get together and form the Abalone Alliance, which was primarily based on using nonviolent direct action as a means of stopping nuclear power in the State of California.

"Since then, I have been doing nonviolent training sessions and a number of other activities with the Abalone Alliance, but I think the nonviolent training sessions have been my most powerful experience, both as an individual and as a woman, helping people to find their own centers of power. Sometimes we've had twenty-five or fifty people getting together who just have a vague sense of something wrong and who want to do something, but have no catalyst for action. In the course of a day, through the experience of nonviolence training, I've seen these diverse individuals come together, talking together, in small groups—sharing feelings and understanding that together we can change things.

"One of the things that has struck me about this movement is that the Alliance and similar organizations around the country are very compatible with feminism in its ideals, which include decentralization, empowerment, making decisions by consensus.

"One of the finest experiences that I have had in recent months was going to jail with sixteen other women. This was a result of getting arrested on August 6, 1978, at a demonstration against the Diablo Canyon nuclear plant. The group of us decided that we would not take probation, we would not pay fines, we did not want to cooperate with the system in any manner. Consequently, all sixteen of us women found ourselves locked together in a cell for the next nine days. Rather than being intimidated, the experience was quite powerful and we found that even though we were jammed together in a cell not much more than ten by twelve feet, we were able to take good care of each other. We started out by telling each other our life stories, and then we did workshops. We weren't allowed phone calls, we weren't allowed medicine, we weren't allowed books; nevertheless the experience just kept getting better and better.

"One woman had been to the People's Republic of China and told us a story about China each day. Though we clamored for more, she strung it out—Arabian Nights style. Another woman taught us Tai Chi warmup exercises. We would do our Tai Chi exercises every morning, and hear about China; I would talk about the Abalone Alliance, and different women shared their particular skills. But that type of experience really typifies what I perceive as the ideals of the Abalone

Alliance—which are certainly not always lived up to—but that kind of support, that kind of community, that kind of energy we had of moving together through an experience and taking our lives into our own hands."

Empowerment, decentralization, and the consensus process are concepts we share in articulating the vision of Women in the Wilderness. "Empowerment" could be leadership, the crux of which is becoming the leader of your own life. One can't really "lead" anyone else's life. In fact the true leader is subtle, content to point the way, to create an environment in which others can tap into the leadership within themselves. The true leader refuses followers and insists that all persons must find their own way; not only find it but discover that they are capable of doing so. For women leadership is hindered by low self-esteem and lack of self-confidence. Overcoming this is a lonely struggle. These are some of the values we share with some of the environmental activists.

Another panelist, Gayle Rosencrantz, attorney, a mother of five, and a member of the board of directors of Friends of the Earth, tells us:

"Six years ago, I was very typical of most Americans. I didn't think about nuclear power and if someone asked me about it I would think, Well, it's clean, cheap, and the answer to all our problems. I did not know the problems with radioactivity and waste and I think that most of us in the United States at that time were in the same situation. It was a well-kept secret. The dangers and the unresolved problems of nuclear waste were confined to the boardrooms, and the public heard only what the industry and Nuclear Regulatory Commission wanted us to hear, which wasn't very much.

"In my own life, I had tried a lot of things. I thought I would find fulfillment in my marriage and I discovered that that was an illusion; and I thought that having five children would be fulfilling but I discovered that I couldn't find it through them; luckily my children are all very individualistic and they wouldn't let me get away with that approach. I tried volunteer work; I went to law school, I became a very successful lawyer; but always I was very dissatisfied, and searching, searching.

"In the fall of 1974, after trying all sorts of things, my husband and I attended an introductory weekend seminar in the Santa Cruz Mountains given by the Creative Initiative Foundation, and we experienced something which changed our lives; we learned a little bit about ourselves, how our conditioning keeps us from seeing the reality around us, and we started an educational process which incorporates the principles of the world's great religions, learning them and understanding what they mean.

"Shortly after this I was invited to dinner by some people and they

Currently, 16 mills in the U.S. process 10 to 15 million tons of ore annually, producing almost eight million tons of tailings. In addition, poorer ores will be exploited as deposits are depleted, leaving a higher proportion of tailings for each pound of useable uranium.

Uranium represents less than one percent of the ore that is removed from the ground and processed. Considerable amounts of non-uranium radioactive materials, such as thorium, radon, and radioactive lead, are left behind. In fact, 85 percent of the radioactivity remains after the ore is processed.

The Nuclear Regulatory Commission (NRC) for years asserted that the effects of radon emitted by tailings piles need only be considered for one year. These estimates are now being revised to 80,000 to 100,000 years. In 1978, the NRC admitted that new studies indicate radon releases increase with time.

Mill tailings in Grand Junction, Colorado, were found to be releasing three times more radon than when dumped ten years earlier. Not surprisingly, Mesa County, where Grand Junction is located, has a rate of acute leukemia twice that of the state as a whole. . . .

There are about 140 million tons of tailings piled around the country, most in the Rocky Mountain states. These are huge, dusty heaps up to a mile long and 70 feet high. They are active pollutants for hundreds of thousands of years. Their poisons are dispersed over hundreds of acres by wind, rain, snow, and erosion.

—IRENE FUERST,
"Not Man Apart,"
Friends of the Earth,
February 1980

started to talk to me about nuclear power and my reaction was, 'Well, what's wrong? What's the problem?' This was the spring of 1974. And I was given a brief education about it, referred to several books; but I was just given statistics. And I will never forget two very important facts that influenced me. One is that plutonium remains radioactive for hundreds of thousands of years, and that struck me. You know, our agricultural society is only ten thousand years old; how many civilizations will rise and fall in two hundred thousand years? Who's going to take on the responsibility of guarding those wastes from our children and thousands of generations to come? And then the other thing that struck me was the fact that radioactivity not only kills, by causing cancer and illness, but it destroys the genetic integrity of our species and all living things. It has taken twenty billion years, science estimates, to develop the information that is hidden in the genetic code. In no time at all radioactivity can disturb and alter this basic information of the species.

"In a short time I became involved in environmental movements. Until that time I had not been involved in any causes. I had been involved in making money, working hard, and making it in the business community. This opened my eyes and for the first time I realized that we are all related to one another; we are all interconnected; we are all interdependent, and what I do in San Francisco today can have an impact in Brazil thousands of years from now. This is a closed system that we live in and everything that everybody does has an effect on everyone else. None of us can escape that—regardless of nationalities, religions, races; none of that has any bearing whatsoever, and it's high time that all of us realized it and lived that way. Suddenly I became very involved in the antinuclear movement.

"I became the president and chairman of the board of Project Survival and I went on the board of directors for Friends of the Earth. But during the two years from the spring of 1974 until June of 1976, when the Nuclear Initiative was brought forth in California, I devoted my whole focus to getting the initiative on the ballot, and then getting it to the public and getting it passed. Well, it wasn't passed, but it accomplished a great deal. In January, 1975, nobody knew anything about nuclear power. You could open a newspaper and find nothing there. After our campaign, in June, 1976, it came out in the open; the subject of nuclear power was no longer a secret. The world knew about it, the whole country knew about it. And since that time criticism of nuclear power has increasingly gained credibility and respectability due to our efforts here in California.

"I learned a few things during that campaign—one is that individuals do make a difference. The fact that we could work on this, get it on the ballot, get the issue out in the open, is tremendous progress. The other thing that I learned was that I'm just as much of an expert as anybody else, if I set my mind to it. Like most people in this room I thought, 'Well, I'm nobody; who am I? I'm not a scientist, I'm not a nuclear physicist, what do I know? How can I decide?' But I realized that this is an issue that everyone has to become informed on. Everyone is affected by it, therefore, everyone should have a say in it.

"This is not just an issue for scientists—in fact, it's very dangerous if you leave an issue like this to the so-called experts. The only solution is for everybody to be informed, to work together, to have input into the decision-making process, and to demand that we be part of the decision-making process because there is no leader out there who is going to save us. We have to do it ourselves. We have to inform ourselves. We have to take action and take responsibility. This is our hope and the only hope."

Stephanie Mills, assistant editor of *Coevolution Quarterly:* "What interests me about nuclear power is that the opposition to it is illuminating alternative energy systems which are very conducive to a decentralist society.

"I'm a generalist about issues: energy concerns me, genetic diversity concerns me, aesthetics concern me. The world gets uglier by the minute because the lives we lead consume more—whether it's nuclear, wood, or coal. The energy issue gives us a window on social reorganization and it fits into a lot of other questions about how we consume and produce. When any system grows beyond a certain scale, it goes haywire. Systems can get too large to control, and I think the nuclear power system is a prime example. It's on a scale of capital consumption, promised output, demand for expertise, that's way beyond popular control.

"I believe that there is a great hope for turning around the idea that nuclear power is going to be a useful way for us to get energy. Nuclear power is electricity. Only 13 percent of the energy we use is in the form of electricity. This is a major fact and an often overlooked point on this debate. It's not back to the caves without the nuclear plant.

"But I am interested in the waste problem. The waste issue is a real one—it's a serious issue. We haven't been civilized as long as we are going to have to take care of all this radioactive material. Even if the plants are eventually decommissioned and we figure out how to get enough concrete to bury the fuel rods or dismantle the paraphernalia, we are going to have to deal with the wastes. That's the problem— and the way to deal with the problem we've produced here is to build better people, starting with ourselves. We are going to have to have incredible taboos and very responsible people to look after these wastes, generation after generation. Likewise, ideas like planting trees, maintaining gardens, and carrying on restoration activities for the whole

The decision of a consortium of Ohio utility companies to abandon construction of four major nuclear power plants has been dubbed the largest such cancellation in the history of the nuclear industry.

[A] key reason for dropping the project was said to be a smaller demand for electricity than had been expected.

More than 50 other power plants across the U.S. have reportedly been cancelled since 1972, and decline in the rate of growth in demand for electricity has been a factor in some.

Several recent studies have held out conservation, or more efficient use of energy, as the first-priority solution to the nation's energy problems.

The latest study of the Three Mile Island mishap ought to erase any doubts that such caution is warranted. An investigative team discovered that the Three Mile Island accident came much closer—within 30 to 60 minutes—to a catastrophic "meltdown" of the nuclear fuel core than had previously been reported. The Special Study Group faulted the Nuclear Regulatory Commission.

This new study was conducted for the NRC. It reached the disturbing conclusion that the NRC was not so much "badly managed" as it "wasn't managed at all," and it warned that as presently constituted the NRC is incapable of managing a safety program "adequate to ensure the public health and safety."
—Christian Science Monitor,
January 29, 1980

planet are going to be important. We've taken on a planetary responsibility, like it or not, to do something about this waste and to rebuild the earth. I don't see how we can do that until we start from within and begin to suffer with the earth—have a basic compassion for our own biology.

"I have very little faith in the federal government and state governments because I think they are inherently outsized. An entity like the federal government, no matter how good or how earnest the people in it are and how good the lobbyists that are trying to furnish it information are, is forced to generalize so much about situations that are specific, personal and local, that inevitably it does a bad job. That's why I think it doesn't matter who is President. It's impossible to do the job well.

"High technology, like nuclear power, is impossible to run democratically. There is never going to be democratic nuclear power. It requires a grid system and ensures that people are going to be dependent on a centralized system. It doesn't matter who owns it— dependency is an essential part. An alternative is to look to see if a solution can be managed at a neighborhood level. Scale is key."

Dorothy Hughes—mother of eight, director of the Marin Mental Health Association, member of the board of directors of the Abalone Alliance—spoke next:

"I have been concerned about living in a democracy where people don't vote, in a country where people are educated but nobody thinks and everyone blindly plays follow the leader. As head of a mental health association, I keep wondering who's crazy.

"I began to explore the antinuclear movement and saw that it expressed many of my concerns about health, ecology, disarmament, employment and inflation, civil liberties, and decentralized grassroots government. I went to an Abalone Alliance conference, and although it was a very young movement, here was a group of people who really knew how to get things done. Sometimes it was agonizing; we were doing things by consensus which can be very slow and difficult; but it has great merit for those of us who still believe in democracy. You have to coax and urge people along, respect and include the differences of opinion. Eventually you will get the best of the group and you end up with people firmly committed. People don't go off saying, 'I didn't vote for it,' or 'I'm not going to do it.'

"It provides me an opportunity to work in an effective way, with gentleness and caring. These are qualities that many men would like to have in their work also. They have had less of an opportunity to work in this manner. It provides an opportunity for women to use their minds and to begin to turn away from some of the faulty assumptions on which much of our scientific and technological knowledge has been based. In the Abalone Alliance there are no leaders in the old sense. It is a primarily nonhierarchical movement, based on respect for the individual and an understanding that individuals working cooperatively are what make it move. We attempt to keep things small and local, networking rather than building a traditional hierarchy. My work with the alliance has provided me as a woman with ways to avoid playing into sexism, racism, and oppression.

"There are increasing numbers of grassroots movements, all over the country, that are exploring alternative technologies—wind, solar, biomass, geothermal, just to mention a few. These groups look at what resources are available in the community. What's appropriate. It's a very local way of looking at the energy problem. This is a very exciting time in my life."

The Abalone Alliance is just one of a dozen or so "alliances" that have sprung up around the country to oppose nuclear power. There is a Clamshell Alliance, Crabshell Alliance, Nautilus Alliance, Cactus Alliance, Lone Star Alliance, Sunbelt Alliance, Palmetto Alliance, and Catfish Alliance, to mention a few regional networks. These are autonomous groups, some more organized and active than others, loosely affiliated by virtue of a common network of people who value the land and our relationship with the Earth.

The panel concludes. The confluence of our viewpoints is exciting, and there are more women like these panelists now active elsewhere in the environmental movement. We come together from different places but our assumptions are profoundly similar. Men who share these concerns continue to emerge. There were several in the audience for this panel.

From the panel discussion it was obvious to me that the next step was to attend the upcoming demonstration against the opening of the Diablo Canyon nuclear plant in the Big Sur country of San Luis Obispo, California. I take my oldest son.

The day of the demonstration at Diablo Canyon comes. I awaken at three-forty-five in the morning, get Matthew up, dress, eat, and ride south with a busload of Alliance people, some of them friends and neighbors. Three hot air balloons rise slowly in the morning light over valley orchards. We arrive to find a crowd that eventually grows to forty thousand over the course of the afternoon. The sun beats down, monitors argue with people as they try to get them to sit down in front, a woman on stage translates in sign language behind each speaker or singer. Kites flutter in the wind and a pale moon appears in the eastern sky. Governor Jerry Brown makes a surprise appearance and promises to close Diablo down; he receives a roaring approval. Feelings run high. My son lies on the ground next to me as I sit listening. How rarely do we have moments like this anymore! Here is a manchild, half

Hawaii Electric signed a $200 million contract for the world's first wind farm, designed to produce roughly 10 percent of the electricity of Oahu. Wind experts predict that with a crash program 10 to 20 percent of the total electrical energy of the U.S. could be produced by wind energy by the year 2000.

grown, to whom I gave birth fifteen years ago. His generation and his children's will bear the brunt of these decisions that we make now. Windsocks whip in the gusty wind; bright batik banners snap and flutter. An energy fair goes on with demonstration of solar panels and windmill nearby. What will the world be like for them?

The speakers continue. A San Luis Obispo resident recalls the growth of opposition to Diablo. The county commission was meeting to discuss the Diablo plant. Mothers from all over town came in to protest the meeting, displaying pictures of their children, saying, "This is what it's all about." That summer of 1977, forty-seven people occupied the plant and were arrested for trespassing. The following summer, 478 people were arrested in the continued protest against the plant's construction. Following the Three Mile Island accident, thirty thousand people rallied at City Hall in San Francisco, and forty thousand people attend today's demonstration in San Luis Obispo. "We are part of a people's movement around the world," says a speaker from the American Friends Service Committee. Fifty thousand people marched in Germany carrying banners that said, "We all live in Harrisburg."

During the previous summer's occupation of Diablo, participants sent up helium balloons with notes attached saying, "RADIATION CAN REACH YOU AS EASILY AS DID THIS BALLOON." Balloons were found hundreds of

Diablo Canyon Rally, 1977

Diablo Canyon Rally, 1979

miles away in the mountains. Today we release more balloons, blue, red, yellow, green, with the same message attached.

A woman who had been arrested in last summer's protest speaks: "We have been convicted for trespassing. Yes, we are guilty of concern for human life. We'd rather have our bodies in jail than our consciences in prison."

Daniel Ellsberg is a firebrand; he speaks and the crowd grows silent. "We are here to exercise the first amendment right to dissent, to disobey illegitimate authority. Nuclear power is the religion of male chauvinism, the rape of nature and the cult of leadership." His intensity is startling. He recalls an incident in which an interviewer asked him how it felt to be considered a traitor. Ellsberg shot back, "This country was founded by traitors." Skepticism of authority, especially of politicians, is part of the American tradition. There is no place to run, no place to hide from the realities of nuclear waste and radiation, he assures everyone. "Balloons released from Rocky Flats in Colorado were found in Indiana."

Singer Holly Near's statement echoes my own feelings: "There is no difference between the personal and the political. We need to put our energy into saving our Mother Earth." Following her, near the end of the demonstration, a small group of Indians comes on stage.

Bill Wahpepah of the American Indian Movement asks for silence as a group performs a brief traditional ceremony for us. A woman's high wail rises in the afternoon as the others beat the drums. After the ceremony Bill speaks:

"Finally you are beginning to learn what the Indians have been trying to tell you all along. We do not own the land, the land owns us. We, the people, are the truth of this land. We are the power, we have let this political system go too far. We must take life back into our own hands.

"Where are the people of color here today? We are not a movement until we are all here together; chicanos, women, blacks . . . all peoples. We are not the savages white society would make us out to be.

"It is an honor to speak with you, even if you only understand one-half of what I say. The other half you have to learn. Take it in your hands and work. And remember that we are all the children of our Mother Earth." His words hit home. My son Matt puts his arm around me. It is time to go.

Children, whether our own or others, provide us with a touchstone for our decisions about technology and the future. One has only to stop for a moment and ask, "What will this leave for the children, and their children's children?" Against this criterion it is easy to see the folly of radioactive wastes, mining of fossil fuels, and agricultural practices that erode the topsoil, which takes eight hundred years to make one inch.

Like the Pilgrims long ago, the children and I begin Thanksgiving with the Indians. At seven-thirty in the morning we board the ferryboat to Alcatraz Island in San Francisco Bay to join some of the Native Americans in celebration of the occupation of Alcatraz ten years ago. For many Native Americans Alcatraz is a symbol of the way they find themselves imprisoned and isolated by our system. It has become a focal point for the American Indian Movement. Their occupation of the island was inspired by the Fort Laramie treaty of 1868, which says that all federal lands not in use will revert back to the original people, the American Indians.

We walk up the road on the hills of Alcatraz, a rag-taggle lot—TV and radio reporters, Indians, blacks, whites, women, men, park rangers, children, drumming and chanting. A Japanese Buddhist monk brings up the rear with a drum and a chant of his own that blends in with the high-pitched chant of the Indians. The ceremony begins as the Native Americans form a circle. More drumming and seven pipes are lit, one by one, offered to the four directions, and passed among the Indians who occupied Alcatraz ten years ago. They dance slowly in the circle, wearing the sacred Indian colors, red, white, yellow, and black, the colors of all people. Letters are read from three Native Americans in prison waiting trial in Los Angeles. The empty prison cells of Alcatraz echo back the drumbeats, constant now, and louder as we stand, circled in silence. We are foolish if we fail to listen to these voices.

"It's time we all become Native Americans," says the poet Gary Snyder, "and live with a sense of belonging here." The struggle of the Native Americans, the traditional people, is our struggle also. It is a struggle not only for health and future generations but is also a struggle for the sacramental view of the world.

It is important to note that much of the world's uranium lies under sacred lands of native peoples such as the Aborigines in Australia and the American Indians on our own continent. As an Indian friend pointed out to me, somehow the ancient people knew these lands had special powers and so made them sacred.

The destruction of sacred lands for uranium mining unleashes the deadliest powers known to humankind. Here is the real fall from grace, the trespassing in the garden that will turn the Earth into a hell for us all. A nuclear holocaust will be a destruction of the world by fire. Only a return to a sacramental view of nature, which includes ourselves and all beings, be they plant, animal, or mineral, will give us the life and hope we have been entrusted with for all generations to come.

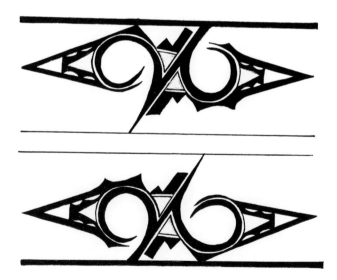

VIII   Everything for a Safe Voyage

VIII

Everything for a Safe Voyage
*in your own backyard, where to begin,
a directory of programs and outfitters, resources
and organizations*

rom the Grand Canyon to Alcatraz, one never knows where the journey will end. But for the last few years, Women in the Wilderness has served as a point of departure for these explorations. The organization exists to protect and support our kinship with the natural world and to help women assume leadership roles both in our own lives and societally. How can it work for you?

It's important to understand that Women in the Wilderness is the seed of a process, one that can grow inside of you, or in your own backyard. Whether you live in the city or the country, the natural world is still home; we depend upon her totally for our sustenance and life. Where does the water you drink come from? The food you eat? Begin to think about it for a moment. Begin to reconnect with the natural world; wherever you are, you can make the connection in a variety of ways, but the first step is to go outside.

Do you know where the nearest public park is and how to get there? Cities and counties have park departments that can furnish this information, so do state and federal governments. Contact them. What plants and trees grow in your neighborhood? What birds and animals live nearby? Which species live there year round and which migrate?

If you have a backyard, you can sleep in it to begin with. Watch the moon, learn its phases. At what point does your own menstrual flow begin? Some women can tell their cycles by the moon. Can you? Go for a walk under a full moon with a friend. Start a garden, even if you've only got a windowsill. Learn how things grow.

Celebrate the traditional Earth festivals or solstices and equinoxes which mark the beginnings of the four seasons. Summer solstice falls around June 21 and is the longest day of the year. Winter solstice comes about December 21 and is the longest night of the year. At the equinoxes, day and night are of equal duration. The spring equinox falls around

We see ruby-crowned kinglets, black scoters, pigeon guillmots, pelicans, cormorants, murres, western gulls, terns, and brown towhees.

March 20 and the fall equinox on September 22. The date will vary slightly from year to year. Many calendars give these dates each year and note the phases of the moon.

A very helpful book for this is *Earth Festivals, Seasonal Celebrations for Everyone Young and Old*, by Dolores La Chapelle and Janet Bourgne. It can be ordered from Finn Hill Arts, Publisher ($10.95), P.O. Box 542, Silverton, Colorado 81433. Dolores La Chapelle has also written another good book, *Earth Wisdom* ($9.95), which can be ordered from the Guild of Tutors Press, 1019 Gayley Avenue, Los Angeles, California 90024.

If you're interested in more challenging activities, remember to start simply. You don't have to have money, organizations, and long vacations; just begin to notice the world around you. Reconnect. Begin with an outdoor activity that you feel comfortable with. This could be anything from plant identification and birdwatching to technical rock climbing. Include your friends, and someone who is skilled in that activity. A small group of women on the East Coast who organized around the idea of Women in the Wilderness met monthly for a potluck supper to plan an outing. Their activities have included a wildflower walk, a day of cross-country skiing, a winter overnight, and an occasional fireside chat. This is simply an informal group of friends who enjoy outdoor activities and learning new skills together. Expenses are shared among the group, as well as equipment upon occasion. By pooling together, transportation costs are kept to a minimum.

This kind of informal organizing follows the "common adventurer" concept. It's a do-it-yourself method for getting out. There are no formal leaders as such, just an organizer or originator who suggests the idea for an outing. Those who are interested get together and make a group decision as to what will be done, for how long. Each person is responsible for herself and relies on the other members of the group to be also. Everyone is expected to carry her own weight, literally. The idea is to encourage people to learn at their own pace, plan their own adventures, and learn by doing.

Here are a few words of caution if you want to use the "common adventurer" concept. I repeat, be sure to include someone in your group who has some basic skills and someone who has some basic first-aid knowledge. Choose an activity well within the abilities already available in your group. More explicitly, if you have a group of women none of whom has spent much time outdoors, you might start with planning a weekend morning walk at your nearest park, where you can be guided by a ranger or park services employee, where maps are furnished that are easy for a beginner to read, and where trails are clearly marked. A two- to three-mile walk might be plenty of distance for a beginning group to cover comfortably. Take your time; be sure everyone in your group is cared for. Set your pace at the level of your slowest member. Stay within sight of one another. The following guidelines apply to outdoor activities from the simplest to the most complicated levels and for any outing beyond your local park. If you go off for a more extended experience, these same principles apply.

Start with friends meeting beforehand. Decide on a common goal. Mix experienced and inexperienced people and allow time for those who are inexperienced to learn new skills. Pick resource people carefully. Those will be people who know first aid, and will include someone who has a knowledge of the area you're going into. Have maps; be able to use them and a compass. Plan for the weather to change and carry some kind of rain protection. Always carry water and some minimal amount of food, even on a morning walk. Give your itinerary to someone who is staying behind and tell her when you expect to get back, approximately. Know where you would have to go to get help in case of emergency. That could be anywhere from an easy half-hour hike on a trail to a day's trek across the desert. Use your common sense and think your plan through.

Another way to become active in the out of doors is to go with a professional guide or organization, and the practicalities and safety items will be taken care of for you. But, unless you take part in a program designed to teach you these skills, you won't learn as much as if you do it yourself. However, not everyone wants or needs the outdoor skills; and it's great to have the experience of going on the variety of trips available today. Both kinds of experiences are valuable. I could never learn all the skills I might enjoy having, so while I might organize a small group of friends for some local, easy-to-reach activity, chances are I would go with an outfitter or established program if I wanted to experience dog sledding in Alaska, for example. Choices like these depend on your own level of skill and the skills of your friends. The important thing to remember is to start small, with where you are, who you are, and what you've got. Be realistic about what you know and don't know.

There are some basic principles of outdoor activities that apply anywhere. Be a wise traveler; you will always have an impact on our environment, but you can minimize the effect of your visit by following these suggestions: Stay on marked trails. Travel light; carry only what

It is late as we start on our journey. A thousand stars pierce the night sky as the full moon softens the darkness. Deer! A hundred miles from the city the deer begin to appear . . . one, then two, then fields ablaze with startled eyes riveting on our passing. Each new meadow alive with these graceful creatures adds to my growing intoxication with the night.

—SHERRY DWYER

you need. Leave no trace. Carry out your garbage and trash. Learn how to dispose of your body waste properly. Different terrain requires different measures.

Another good rule is to take only memories and pictures, and leave only footprints, if that! Make drawings if you like, paint, but don't collect. In some areas it is illegal to take even a rock out of the area. You will probably learn more about a natural object in its setting.

There are many books available on safety, low-impact camping, and all manner of outdoor activities. Learn good conservation practices. There are some books and articles on camping with your children. They're rarely too young to take along on a well-planned outing. Lynn Thomas, another Women in the Wilderness member, is finishing a book on women and backpacking. Watch for it. The following are a few of the basic books available now in outdoors stores:

Colin Fletcher, *The New Complete Walker, The Joys and Techniques of Hiking and Backpacking*, 2nd edition. New York: Alfred Knopf, 1974. $10.95.
John Hart, *Walking Softly in the Wilderness*, Sierra Club Guide to Backpacking, 1977. $5.95.
Harvey Manning, *Backpacking One Step at a Time*. New York: Random House, 1973. $2.95.

Something else that must be kept in mind if you go for anything longer than a short dayhike is the subject of fires. Know whether or not a campfire is permitted in the area where you're traveling. Learn about fire building from an experienced guide. Know how to use and repair a cookstove before going on any outing with one. Many wilderness areas require camping permits and permits to build fires. Some areas are too fragile to allow fires. Observe the rules! Fire can travel underground, spreading through root systems, even after you think you've put it out. Knowing how, when, and where to have a fire is essential. Knowing how to determine whether or not a fire is completely out is crucial. Don't just read about this in a book; learn from someone who knows and has a sense of responsibility and kinship with the land.

The Forest Service and the National Park Service issue the permits. Be responsible; find out beforehand if you need one. Contact the Forest Service or the National Park Service in your region. They have offices throughout the country. Contact the regional office nearest you. Contact your State Park system as well. The government and the American Red Cross both put out a range of good, free information on wilderness travel and safety.

Equipment and clothing catalogs can dazzle you with an array of items for any and all occasions. Hold off on making purchases, especially if you're new to getting out. Learn the merits and drawbacks of, say, a PolarGuard versus a down sleeping bag. Tents can be rented. Often sleeping bags can be rented. Or you may borrow from a friend, if you take care of the bag and have it cleaned properly before returning it. Other sources of less-expensive equipment are do-it-yourself kit companies and seconds stores. Seconds stores carry only manufacturers' seconds and offer good buys in parkas, sleeping bags, tents, miscellaneous gear, and clothing. Here are a few that I've heard about. I'm sure there are more.

EASTERN MOUNTAIN STORES
BARGAIN BASEMENT
1041 Commonwealth Avenue
Boston, MA 02215
(617) 254–4250

NORTH FACE FACTORY OUTLET
1238 Fifth Street at Gilman
Berkeley, CA 94710
(415) 526–3530

COLORADO OUTDOORS
1205 G West Elizabeth
Ft. Collins, CO 80521
(303) 484–7086

SECONDS BEST
2042 Fourth Street
San Rafael, CA 94901
(415) 457–5544

MOUNTAIN MISER
6238 East Euclid
Englewood, CO 80111
(303) 757–2947

SONOMA OUTFITTERS
608 Mendocino Avenue
Santa Rosa, CA 95401
(707) 528–1920

Often manufacturers sell boys' cuts as women's clothing. Look and ask for *women's* clothing. More and more manufacturers are producing women's clothing and equipment actually cut for women's bodies.
L. L. Bean of Freeport, Maine, open 24 hours a day, 365 days a year, with an excellent mail-order service, has a large selection of women's outdoor wear.

We've heard good things about Outdoor Gal, a mail-order clothing operation for the outdoor woman at 116 East Chestnut Street, Burlington, Wisconsin 53105.

OUTFITTERS AND PROGRAMS
OFFERING ALL-WOMEN'S COURSES

There can be quite a difference between a program offered by a group whose business is doing women's trips (of which there are very few) and one by an organization that includes one or more women's programs in its offerings. Feminist consciousness will most likely influence the former; the latter may simply be a standard trip run by women who still use a traditional leadership model.

Very few organizations focus on actually teaching skills. Most offer

Can you live a full life cautiously?
—BARBARA HAZILLA

outdoor experiences with skill building as a secondary purpose, which depends on your own initiative. Palisades School of Mountaineering in California does teach a women's climbing course; the National Outdoor Leadership School in Wyoming, using a traditional leadership model, teaches a women's mountaineering course; Outward Bound schools focus more on an intense wilderness experience than on skills building. Both NOLS and OB are still hindered by their origins as military survival training, though their programs are very respectable. Check the literature *carefully* and find out whether you're getting into a teaching situation which demands a high level of participation, builds skills, and can be great fun, or signing up for a tour with all your meals prepared for you and guides rowing you down the river while you watch the scenery go by.

The following organizations or programs offer at least one all-women's trip during the course of their year. Few programs offer trips only for women. The majority are geared to a mixed audience and include a women's trip among a variety of other programs.

Neither Women in the Wilderness nor I, China Galland, assume any liability by listing these organizations in this directory. It is intended as a resource list and guide to women's programs. Current program schedules and prices are available by writing to the following addresses:

AMERICAN WOMEN'S HIMALAYAN EXPEDITIONS (AWHE)
1013 Paradise Way; Palo Alto, CA 94306
Supports the participation of women in expeditionary mountaineering. Funds left from the 1978 women's Annapurna Expedition will be used as grants or loans to women taking part in climbing expeditions and exchange programs with women climbers from other countries, and for summer meets.

ARTEMIS
P.O. Box 5749; Austin, TX 78763
Chartered adventures available to most areas of the Southwest. A small company which organizes back-country trips for women in small groups who explore rivers, mountains, and deserts, acquiring basic outdoor skills and experience. In the summer, Artemis goes to the mountains of New Mexico, Colorado, and Wyoming. Winter, they use the rivers and mountains of Big Bend, Texas.

BLACKBERRY CREEK CAMP
P.O. Box 28; Pulga, CA 95965
(916) 334–9720
A residential summer camp for young women nine through fifteen years of age, run by an all-female staff. Situated in a rural community

Finding my own way is more challenging. I become more alert and attentive, more animal-like. The rocky faces have a magnetic pull for me. I scramble up on all fours. Playing with the limits of what I can do without the safety of ropes or companions. Tuning ever more finely the interplay between visual perception and kinesthetic sensing. My eyes see a path up a rock. Is it do-able? There is no one to tell me this, or make suggestions about the "right" way to do it. Just the rock— and to dialogue with the rock, I must climb it. Always at some risk. I get totally absorbed and present as I feel my way up the rock. And very alive.

—BARBARA HAZILLA

in northern California and surrounded by national forest, Blackberry Creek Camp aims to promote self-confidence, self-reliance, and emotional growth through outdoor group living. Swimming, day and overnight hikes. Campers also learn basic tool use, farm animal care, organic gardening (much of the camp's food comes from its gardens), canning, cheese and yogurt making, and may choose from a variety of activities such as pottery making, dyeing, and weaving. Vegetarian food provided.

ENCOUNTER FOUR
Kayla Melville
Butler County Community College; Butler, PA 16001
(412) 287–8711, ext. 138
Adventure-based outdoor program for a variety of people. Women's courses include cross-country skiing, winter camping, rock climbing, white-water rafting and canoeing, flatwater canoeing, caving, and backpacking. These trips led by women are in groups of eight to twelve participants of varied age and experience.

GIRL SCOUTS OF AMERICA
830 Third Avenue; New York, NY 10022
(212) 940–7500
Founded in 1912 by Juliette Gordon Low, the Girl Scouts is the largest voluntary organization for girls in the world. Open to all girls, ages six to seventeen, Girl Scouts provides outdoor opportunities through camping experiences right from the start. Courses vary from camping, backpacking, mountain climbing, cross-country skiing, rafting, canoeing to survival and desert travel. They operate camps in all the mountain ranges of the United States. An excellent way to start early.

HEALING WAYS FOR WOMEN
P.O. Box 350; Guerneville, CA 95446
Biannual gatherings in the redwoods of Sonoma. For women healers, artists, musicians, and friends, providing an opportunity to express and explore the image of the goddess. The weekend includes workshops, recreation, vegetarian food, indoor lodging, and child care.

THE INFINITE ODYSSEY
25 Huntington Avenue, Suite 324; Boston, MA 02116
(617) 353–1793
Among their offerings is a women's rafting and mountaineering trip in the Tetons of Wyoming. Designed and led by women, the course offers instruction in rope work, rock climbing, orienteering, and minimum-impact camping.

INSTITUTE FOR ENVIRONMENTAL AWARENESS
Women's Programs: Bertha Petruski
P.O. Box W-821; Greenfield, MA 01302
The guiding purpose of the institute is to develop awareness, understanding, and positive action toward both the natural and cultural environments among people of all ages and circumstances. They use the philosophies and skills of conservation, outdoor and environmental education. The institute has a wide variety of programs especially for women, ranging from climbing and orienteering to "The Night Experience" and "Counseling and Caring Through Outdoor Programs."

KEEP LISTENING
P.O. Box 446; Sandy, OR 97055
(503) 622–3895
A year-round program of backpacking, bicycle camping, and cross-country skiing trips for women in the Northwest. Sessions teach outdoor skills, so that the beginner can learn what she needs to plan her own trips.

NANTAHALA OUTDOOR CENTER, INC.
Star Route, P.O. Box 68; Bryson City, NC 28713
(704) 488–2175
The center is open year round, offering a wide range of adventurous outdoor experiences to people with all ranges of experience. They provide equipment and instruction in a variety of areas, with a large white-water program. Women's skills clinics are offered.

NATIONAL OUTDOOR LEADERSHIP SCHOOL (NOLS)
P.O. Box AA; Lander, WY 82520
(307) 332–4381
Teaches skills essential for the preservation of the earth's wilderness; minimum-impact camping and leadership are essential. Among their offerings is a month-long women's mountaineering course led by women. Emphasis is placed on technical climbing skills, such as steep snow and rock work, protection placement, snow travel techniques, and peak ascents.

NATURE EXPLORATIONS—Tuleyome Peninsula
Conservation Center
1176 Emerson Street; Palo Alto, CA 94301
(415) 324–8737
Nonprofit, tax-exempt organization of teachers, artists, and parents providing active environmental education for people of all ages. Special offerings include women's backpacking trips, a single-parent-family program, and other workshops organized and led by women.

NORDIC SKI VENTURES
P.O. Box 1576; Tahoe City, CA 95730
(916) 583–2875
The creation of two women, both Tahoe ski guides, this small organization offers an in-depth approach to cross-country skiing. Teaches basic cross-country techniques and winter safety skills. One- to five-day programs.

OUTBACK ADVENTURES
Valerie Berg
505 Fruit, N.W.; Albuquerque, New Mexico 87102
(505) 842–6226
This New Mexico-based company provides backpacking-snorkeling adventures to Baja, cross-country skiing in New Mexico, backpacking and rock climbing in New Mexico and Texas, and spring white-water rafting in New Mexico and Colorado. They do contract courses for stress-management and organizational retreats. All trips also offered at various times for women as professional retreats, skills training, or adventure trips. Staffed by skilled wilderness people and psychologists.

OUTDOOR EDUCATION ASSOCIATION
11468 Redwood Highway; Wilderville, OR 97543
(503) 479–4215
In cooperation with Osprey River Trips, Inc., offers some women-only wilderness trips as well as trips for women and men. Experiential white-water training in oar- and paddle-powered inflatable rafts.

THE OUTDOOR WOMAN'S SCHOOL
Carole Latimer
2519 Cedar Street; Berkeley, CA 94708
(415) 848–5189
For women with all degrees of experience. Offers backpacking classes and wilderness trips throughout the year, cross-country skiing and snow camping in winter. The aim is to teach women wilderness skills and make them aware of themselves as physically strong people.

OUTWARD BOUND, INC.
384 Field Point Road; Greenwich, CT 06830
(203) 661–0797   (800) 243–8520 (toll free)
An action-oriented program for personal growth, service to others, and adventure education. It is designed so that students will meet challenging experiences in wilderness settings. Outward Bound operates through seven different schools around the country, all of which have courses for both women and men, including women-only courses and a program for the handicapped.

PALISADE SCHOOL OF MOUNTAINEERING
P.O. Box 694; Bishop, CA 93514
(714) 935–4330
Offers a broad spectrum of mountaineering courses and guided climbs throughout the year, primarily in the Sierra Nevada. A basic mountaineering course for women taught by women, teaching the basic skills needed to climb safely on rock, snow, and glaciers, is offered.

SEAWORTHY WOMEN
2210 Wilshire Boulevard, Suite 254; Santa Monica, CA 90403
(213) 397–7728
Instruction for women from beginning through advanced sailing.
Offers cruises, from one day to one month, to the offshore islands
of California as well as in the Caribbean; combines sea and land
explorations.

SOBEK EXPEDITIONS, INC.
P.O. Box 761; Angels Camp, CA 95222
(209) 736–2661
Specializes in wilderness explorations around the world, pioneering
some rather exotic river runs and expeditions, for men and women.
They are promoting all-women expeditions and hope to sponsor a
major first women's descent of a wild river overseas.

TRAILHEAD VENTURES
P.O. Box CC; Buena Vista, CO 81211
(303) 395–8001
Prime hiking in the Rocky Mountains and the Southwest. Committed
to wilderness preservation, with an emphasis on responsible hiking
and camping techniques, by which humans leave the smallest traces
of their visits. Offers a basic backpacking course for women only.

UNDERWAY
Gail Stepina, Touch of Nature Environmental Center
Southern Illinois University; Carbondale, IL 62901
(618) 457–0348
Courses offered for women only, men only, and women and men.
Backpacking, canoeing, caving, rock climbing, land navigation, and
cross-country skiing in the Ozark Mountains of Illinois, Missouri,
and Arkansas, with special trips to Canada, North Carolina, Texas,
Georgia, Florida, and Wyoming.

UNIVERSITY OF THE WILDERNESS
P.O. Box 1687; Evergreen, CO 80439
(303) 674–9724
Offers women's backpacking and runs canoe, ski touring, and
showshoe trips in various wilderness environments. Also offers
Wilderness Photography workshops.

WASHINGTON WOMEN OUTDOORS, INC.
P.O. Box 301; Garrett Park, MD 20766
(301) 942–8677
Trains metropolitan Washington, D.C., women in a variety of outdoor
activities from September to June. Fall and spring activities include

hiking and bicycling weekends. Winter hosts their most popular program, cross-country skiing; women can learn how to prepare themselves and their skis, as well as learn actual skiing techniques. WWO's most important function is education through identification with skilled women instructors and with skill manuals using women as models and written in nontechnical terms.

WHITE PINE SKI TOURING CENTER

P.O. Box 417; Park City, UT 84060
(801) 336–2055
Concerned with educating the cross-country skier. Offers wide range of instruction, from day lessons and mini tours on the Park City golf course to several days of touring in the High Uintas. Offers trips for women only as well as for mixed groups.

WILDERNESS LEARNING INSTITUTE

Marilyn Mason
2445 Park Avenue South; Minneapolis, MN 55404
(612) 870–1085
The Wilderness Learning Institute is an educational organization blending the challenge of outdoor experiences with other educational styles. Nature and rock climbing can be great teachers of the human experience. In group rock-climbing experiences for novices, professional mountaineers and psychotherapists weave together situations for facing powerlessness and strengths in a safe environment. Days are filled with climbing; the metaphor of the rock climbing is used in fireside discussions at night. Most programs are four days long. There will also be combination climbing and square-rig sailing on Lake Superior. For mixed groups and professionals, this year's format includes a rock-climbing course for women that focuses on competitiveness, the aspect of ourselves that we so often deny.

WOMEN OUTDOORS

474 Boston Avenue; Medford, MA 02155
(617) 628–2525
A regional network of women who want to develop an integrated, environmentally conscious lifestyle; feel the need to work with nature rather than against it; view wilderness activities as a way in which women can develop power in their own lives; come from all walks of life and touch nature in many different ways. New members and inquiries are welcome.

WOMEN'S SPORTS FOUNDATION
195 Moulton Street; San Francisco, CA 94123
(415) 563–6266
Encourages and supports the participation of women in sports activities. Runs clinics and workshops to improve sports skills, techniques, and knowledge for girls and women. Develops local women's sports associations. Maintains an information and resource center on women's sports.

WOMEN'S WAY SKI SEMINARS
Elissa Sanger
P.O. Box 1182; Tahoe City, CA 95730
(916) 583–2904
Held throughout the winter in various ski areas in California, Colorado, and the East. Five days of instruction in small classes. Before and after skiing, sessions in relaxation, massage, visualization, and body-awareness techniques. Cross country and downhill. Women only.

WOODSWOMEN
3716 Fourth Avenue South; Minneapolis, MN 55409
(612) 823–1900
Operates primarily in Minnesota, Wisconsin, and Ontario, offering guided canoe trips and bike trips for women of all ages and degrees of experience. Vegetarian gourmet camp cooking. Winter camping, skills workshops, and courses on women in the wilderness.

WOMEN IN THE WILDERNESS, INC.
Bldg. 201
Fort Mason; San Francisco, CA 94123
(415) 556–0560

Women in the Wilderness is a lot more than just the organization we've created over the last few years. Like a live current, the name itself energizes something in many women; it speaks to the explorer in us all.

Women in the Wilderness is a process, a vehicle through which women who share an interest in the outdoors and our environment can come to know one another. Like an ecosystem, the network is a community of diverse groups with a variety of needs and interrelationships. The ecosystem, achieving its stability through and because of its diversity, is the natural model to foster. Though science still debates the theory, it makes for a broad kind of common sense. The wilderness itself is the most elaborate example of an ecosystem, able to balance and sustain a welter of complexity and life within itself indefinitely. The wilderness is in fact such an exquisite order that any area left "unmanaged," to its own devices, will return to wilderness.

We envision the growth of autonomous regional groups that will be tied together primarily by our publication. We seek to coordinate efforts nationally and lend mutual support while remaining a regionally based group ourselves. Our network is an attempt to alleviate the problems of top-heavy traditional organizational structures. And, like people, no organization is perfect; we're still in the process of growing, but the network of regional groups fits our belief in the values of self-sufficiency and self-definition, with each group inventing its own size, shape, and focus, based on its own regional mix of women and environment. There is no set way to come together. Through sharing in the network via the publication *Women in the Wilderness* and finding out what works for others, people can get their own ideas about what might fit for them.

In the Bay Area, our program ranges from environmental forums, skills workshops, earthday celebrations such as a summer solstice festival, leadership training workshops, films and slide shows, panel discussion, climbing, running trails, women's drumming workshops, and river trips to painting and photography in the wilderness. It is a wide mix of activities, limited only by the interest of members and the stipulation that all programming must be led by women, though some events are also open to men.

Women in the Wilderness, Outings, Expeditions and Adventures, focuses on special courses from trips for teenagers and school-age children to management executives. We've put on river trips for mothers and daughters, day-long walks in the woods, weekend backpacking, rafting the Grand Canyon, kayaking Baja, and trekking Nepal. Membership is $10 per year and includes a subscription to the quarterly publication. The publication features a directory of outfitters and organizations; a calendar of activities (both our own and others) from around the country; and articles, photographs, and art work on the theme of women and wilderness. The quarterly also carries information about job opportunities in the out-of-doors.

OTHER RESOURCES AND ORGANIZATIONS IN THE NETWORK

The following resources and organizations are those that I know of personally or belong to and have found helpful in either exploring the out-of-doors, learning about the environmental crisis, or documenting a new image of women. This is by no means a complete list of such organizations and doesn't include the very excellent American Friends Service Committee, for example, which has played a major part in the development of many of the organizations listed. These are simply ones with which I have had some personal experience. You will have to add those you know of in your own area.

ABALONE ALLIANCE
452 Higuera Street; San Luis Obispo, CA 95063
One of the several regional-based groups scattered around the country dedicated to a non-nuclear world. Some of the others are: Catfish Alliance, Tallahassee, Fla.; Palmetto Alliance, Columbia, S.C.; Eatern Federation, Washington, D.C.; Friends of the Earth, Woodstock, N.Y.; Clamshell Alliance, Portsmouth, N.H.; Northern Sun Alliance, Minneapolis, Minn.; Sunbelt Alliance, Tulsa, Okla.; Great Plains Federation, Columbia, Mo.; Lone Star Alliance, Austin, Tex.; American Indian Environmental Council, Albuquerque, N. Mex.; Cactus Alliance, Tempe, Ariz.; Rocky Flats Action Group, Denver, Colo.; Headwaters Alliance, Missoula, Mont.; Canadian Coalition for Nuclear Responsibility, Montreal, Canada; Greenpeace, Vancouver, B.C., Canada; Nautilus Alliance, Santa Cruz, Calif.; and the Crabshell Alliance, Seattle, Wash.
These organizations are primarily networks of dedicated volunteers loosely affiliated through common concerns about the dangers of the proliferation of nuclear weaponry and nuclear power.

AMNESTY INTERNATIONAL, USA
304 West 58th Street; New York, NY 10019
Nobel Peace Prize-winning organization, Amnesty International is
a worldwide human rights organization that works on behalf of
prisoners of conscience—those women and men who are in prison
for their beliefs, color, ethnic origin or religion—and opposes the
use of the death penalty and the use of torture in all cases. AI has
adoption groups, letter-writing campaigns, and an active network for
the release of prisoners of conscience and an end to torture worldwide
that you can participate in. Membership also brings news of cases
throughout the world. Participation and membership categories vary.
Donations are tax-exempt. Contact the New York office. This is one
of the most important human rights organizations in existence and
deserves broad support.

BLACK HILLS ALLIANCE
P.O. Box 2508; Rapid City, SD 57701
(605) 342–5127
A coalition of ranchers, environmentalists, and Native Americans
who designed an International Survival Gathering to provide access
to information on alternative energy use and to develop international
strategies to curtail the proliferation of nuclear power and weaponry.
The Black Hills have long been the scene of a bitter struggle over
Indian lands and the interests of uranium and coal mining.

CRANE MOUNTAIN ABBEY
P.O. Box 717; Fairfax, CA 94930
(415) 236–9013
A community of women with the broad purpose of furthering the
integration of the feminine and feminist perspective into our lives
and culture. A nonprofit group, they are currently engaged in a land
search in order to provide a mountain retreat for women in the
wilderness. The word "abbey" was chosen for its connotation of a
spiritual community, since an important part of the group's purpose
involves asking questions about women and spirituality. Since women
have often had little access to land, funds have been raised to purchase
and furnish a wilderness retreat as an essential part of the abbey's
development.

FRIENDS OF THE EARTH
124 Spear Street; San Francisco, CA 94105
Friends of the Earth publishes a very informative newsletter called
Not Man Apart. Subscription is $15 to nonmembers; membership is

$25. FOE also does workshops, publishes books, and has an active membership all over the country dedicated to protection and conservation of our environment.

GREAT EXPEDITIONS
Box 46499, Station G; Vancouver, B.C., Canada V0R467
An information network in Canada that publishes a journal every other month. The journal provides information about nonprofit and noncommercial expeditions, adventure and travel organizations. Also provides information on maps and publications and travel notes on getting around inexpensively, and has personal listings for people planning expeditions. Emphasis is on travel with environmental awareness. One-year subscription is $12 (U.S.). They also maintain a trip log registry for unusual projects, journeys, and experiences, containing first-hand information for would-be explorers.

HASSE & PETRICH
Port Townsend Sails, Point Hudson
315 Jackson; Port Townsend, WA 98368
(206) 385–1640
A company of women sailors and sailmakers experienced in ocean sailing who run their own loft. Their sails have served without fail on the Mediterranean and Caribbean seas, across the Atlantic and Pacific oceans, from the Sea of Cortez to the Gulf of Alaska. They are committed to excellence in design and handcrafted construction in the old world tradition. They make sails for both traditional and modern rigs. Letters, calls, and visitors welcome to the loft.

INDEPENDENT DOCUMENTARY GROUP
161 Vicksburg; San Francisco, CA 94114
(415) 824–5822
A nonprofit, tax-exempt organization of film producers currently working on a feature-length documentary called *Dark Circle* which focuses on the problems of radioactive contamination in America and the role of women in the atomic age. The group is comprised of women and men filmmakers who all consider themselves feminists and who love the wilderness. Other films produced are *Alaska: Land in the Balance* and *Thin Edge of the Bay* on the ecology of San Francisco Bay. Judy Irving, Christopher Beaver, Ruth Landy, Karen Spangenberg, Michael Levin, and Deborah Hoffman are the filmmakers on *Dark Circle.*

THE LIVING MUSIC FOUNDATION, INC.
P.O. Box 68; Litchfield, CN 06759
(203) 567–8796
The Foundation grew out of the experiences and efforts of the Paul Winter Consort. A nonprofit, tax-exempt organization, they are dedicated to using music to enrich the lives of human beings and to awaken a spirit of involvement in the preservation of wildlife and the natural environment. Living Music puts out records, holds educational workshops, events, and benefits, and produces publications, all based on an inclusion of the living sounds of nature and wild beings. Their record *Common Ground* includes the songs of wolves, eagles, and whales. Production is now underway on a recording of sea mammals entitled *Callings*. Events have included expeditions to Baja to play music with the whales and a rafting trip down the Grand Canyon. General membership is $20 and includes newsletters as well as discounts on records and publications; student membership is $10.

MADDUX AND BOLDT PRODUCTIONS
244 West 72nd Street; New York, NY 10023
(212) 724–6678
Women filmmakers filming women out-of-doors. Currently producing a feature-length film on women on a journey into the wilderness, they also have slide shows available of women climbing and women kayaking.

NEW ALCHEMY INSTITUTE
237 Hatchville Road; East Falmouth, MA 02536
(617) 563–2655
A small, international organization dedicated to ecological research and education on behalf of humanity and the planet. The Institute develops solutions to be adopted by individuals or small groups who are trying to create a greener, kinder world. Focus is on ecologically derived forms of energy, agriculture, aquaculture, housing, and landscape. They publish a journal which can be purchased from bookstores or the Institute for $9.95. Membership is $25. Contributions are tax-deductible.

RENDEZ-VOUS HAUTES MONTAGNES
Postfach 15
Telefon 041/94 12 00
CH–6390 Engelberg, Switzerland
A loosely knit international organization of top notch women climbers who meet annually to climb, get acquainted and exchange

information. Members come from the U.S.A., Great Britain, France, Canada, Guatemala, India, Iran, Japan, Australia, Chile, Germany, and most European countries except Rumania, Hungary, Turkey, Albania, Sweden and Ireland. In Switzerland, which has its own Club Suisse de Femmes Alpinists, members formed their group as early as 1918 when the Swiss Alpine Club refused to admit them as members. Mrs. Aline Margot and fourteen other women from Montreaux formed the original group in 1918 which had seven sections only a year later. Over the years the Swiss club has grown to fifty-five sections and eight thousand women members.

WOMEN'S INTERNATIONAL PEACE AND FREEDOM LEAGUE

National Office, U.S.A.
1213 Race Street; Philadelphia, PA 19107
(215) 563–7110

Founded in 1915, WIPFL publishes a fine newsletter that carries a great deal of news on environmental problems and what you can do to help. Subscription is only $4 to nonmembers; membership is $15.

Begun at The Hague in May 1915 in the midst of a world war, women from different countries came together across the battlefields to comfort and strengthen one another, to protest and to plan. Despite the differences in languages and national backgrounds, they founded an international political party for women and men, regardless of creed or color, dedicated to the principles of peace and freedom. Sixty-five years later they have sections all over the world.

What we call the beginning is often the end
And to make an end is to make a beginning.
The end is where we start from.

—T. S. ELIOT,
"Little Gidding," *Four Quartets*

Bibliography

Armstrong, John. *The Paradise Myth*. New York: Oxford University Press, 1969.

Bly, Robert. *Sleepers Joining Hands*. New York: Harper & Row, 1973.

Brown, Dee. *The Gentle Tamers: Women in the Old Wild West*. New York: Putnam, 1968.

Brown, Lloyd. *The Story of Maps*. Boston: Little, Brown, 1950.

Campbell, Joseph. *Hero with a Thousand Faces*. Cleveland: Meridian Books, 1967.

Daly, Mary. *Beyond God the Father*. Boston: Beacon Press, 1973.

————. *Gyn/Ecology*. Boston: Beacon Press, 1978.

David-Néel, Alexandra. *Magic and Mystery in Tibet*. New York: Penguin Books, 1978.

————. *Initiations and Initiates in Tibet*. Berkeley: Shambala Publications, 1970.

Ehrenreich, Barbara, and Dierdre English. *For Her Own Good: 150 Years of the Experts Advice to Women*. New York: Doubleday, Anchor Books, 1979.

Fielder, Leslie. *The Return of the Vanishing American*. New York: Stein & Day, 1969.

Figes, Eva. *Patriarchal Attitudes*. New York: Stein & Day, 1970.

Freeman, Don. "The Computer Labored and Brought Forth a Bear," *TV Guide*, January 1978.

Gherman, Dawn. *From Parlour to Tepee: The White Squaw on the American Frontier*. Ph.D. Dissertation, University of Massachusetts. Ann Arbor: Xerox University Microfilms, 1979. 76–5853.

Griffin, Susan. *Woman and Nature: The Roaring Inside Her*. New York: Harper & Row, 1978.

Halifax, Joan. *Shamanic Voices*. New York: Dutton, 1979.

I Ching. Translated by Richard Wilhelm. New Jersey: Princeton University Press, 1968.

Kopp, Sheldon B. *If You Meet the Buddha on the Road, Kill Him!* New York: Bantam Books, 1976.

Krutch, Joseph Wood. *Baja, The Geography of Hope*. San Francisco: Sierra Club Books, 1967.

La Chapelle, Dolores. *Earth Wisdom*. Los Angeles: Guild of Tutors Press, 1978.

Lerner, Gerda. *The Female Experience: An American Documentary*. Indianapolis: Bobbs Merrill, 1977.

Lovelock, J. E. *Gaia: A New Look at Life on Earth*. New York: Oxford University Press, 1979.

Miller, Luree. *On Top of the World: Five Women Explorers in Tibet*. London: Paddington Press, 1976.

Neumann, Erich. *The Great Mother: An Analysis of the Archetype*. New Jersey: Princeton University Press, Bollingen Series, 1972.

Niethammer, Carolyn. *Daughters of the Earth*. New York: Macmillan, Collier Books, 1977.

Purchas, Samuel. *Purchas His Pilgrimes*. London, 1625.

Ross, Nancy Wilson. *Westward the Women*. New York: Alfred A. Knopf, 1944.

Roszak, Theodore. *Person/Planet*. New York: Doubleday, Anchor Books, 1978.

Sachse, Julius Friedrich. *The German Pietists of Provincial Pennsylvania, 1694–1708*. Philadelphia: Printed for the author, 1895.

Shuttle, Penelope, and Peter Redgrove. *The Wise Wound*. New York: Richard Marek, 1978.

Stephens, James. *A Crock of Gold*. New York: Macmillan, Collier Books, 1974.

Stephenson, E. L. *Portolan Charts*. New York: Hispanic Society, 1911.

Stone, Merlin. *When God Was a Woman*. New York: Dial Press, 1976.

White, Lynn. "The Historical Roots of our Ecological Crisis," *Ecology and Religion in History*. Edited by David and Eileen Spring. New York: Harper & Row, 1974.

Index

Picture Credits